# Selling Your Home

## A Guide For Owners

## Ted Silverman

Layout and design, interior and cover, by the author.

Text set in 11 point Minion Pro.

IIAS

ISBN: 1519335733       ISBN-13: 978-1519335739

Printed in the United States of America

10 9 8 7 6 5 4 3 2 1

# About the Author

Ted Silverman has written on many subjects, from physics and philosophy to economics, history and politics. He is the author of several books, including *Philosophical Solutions: In Physics, Mathematics and the Science of Sentience; Hope and Enterprise: Building a Democratic Economy from Under Ground Up; Economics Laid Bare;* and the forthcoming *Race to Zion: Einstein, Hitler and Dreams of Promised Lands.* His independent work in physics has been published in the proceedings of *SPIE,* the prestigious international organization for optical engineering, where he is regularly invited to speak at professional conferences.

In 1994, Ted and his brother Jerry founded an Internet company, Cybernet, which in 2000 became ACS Sports for a public stock offering. Cybernet and then ACS Sports produced Web sites and television shows for the sports and entertainment industries. Partnerships were created with more than 30 professional sports teams and leagues and many hi-profile individuals and media companies, including the New York Yankees, New York Mets, Baltimore Orioles, Chicago Bears, Denver Broncos, New York Jets, Philadelphia Eagles, MLB, NBA, the Womens' Tennis Association, the Williams sisters, David Bowie, Iman, NBC, the MSG Network, Comcast SportsNet and CBS Radio. Ted personally developed many of the Web sites and together with Jerry managed the digital assets of their hi-profile partners, including the sale of advertising, sponsorships and, in some cases, tickets, via innovative online platforms. They forged precedent-setting online advertising and sponsorship arrangements with Fortune 500 companies such as Verizon and Microsoft, and created the first seven-figure deal for online media rights.

After ACS, Jerry became actively involved in Real Estate and Ted worked on the development of high efficiency, clean energy technologies. Ted was a marketing consultant to Jerry's real estate group from 2003 to 2005, during which time it had $150 million in sales. Ted and Jerry "grew up" in real estate: Their father, trained as an engineer, was a real estate broker and developer, and their mother was actively involved in the management of properties. Ted and Jerry held real estate licenses from young ages, Jerry at 18 and Ted in his early twenties. While assisting Jerry with a real estate marketing campaign, Ted saw an opportunity to accelerate the adoption of home solar energy use by rebating commissions from real estate sales to subsidize solar installations. His idea was to make the transition to solar simple, inexpensive and transparent by offering it to home buyers before they purchase, enabling them to move into an energy efficient home without hassles or large out-of-pocket expenses.

Ted is currently a licensed real estate agent in Maryland and is testing the idea of leveraging the residential real estate point of sale to proliferate home solar energy use.

# Selling Your Home

## Some Introductory Remarks

This little handbook is intended as an easy to use guide for owners of residential real estate who are preparing to sell their home. Unlike other real estate books that may have fallen into the reader's hands, it focuses squarely on a small number of key issues that sellers tend to have trouble with, and makes no pretense of covering every aspect of a home sale. Illustratively, it does not address the decision to sell itself, nor the myriad personal and financial considerations that enter into that decision. On the other hand, the important strategic question of *when* to sell *is* addressed – insofar as it relates to marketing concerns, not to questions of timing that may arise in connection with other issues, such as buying and transitioning to a new home.

Timing is a crucial consideration because, while there are many unpredictable economic factors that determine general market conditions, local real estate markets also vary predictably, on a seasonal basis. All other factors being equal, certain times of the year are more favorable for sellers while others are more favorable for buyers. In this sense, timing is a key marketing issue, especially as it relates to pricing, which, along with timing, entails one of the three most critical marketing decisions a home seller faces – albeit one that many sellers are unprepared to make wisely.

Ironically, the most fundamental marketing issue confronting sellers is rarely even recognized: the venue and method of sale. Most home sellers engage a real estate agent to list their property in the local multiple listing service (MLS) while a few attempt to market their property on their own as a 'FSBO' (For Sale by Owner). In both cases, the same general approach – a negotiated sale – is unconsciously selected. The alternative, which is usually completely overlooked because it is not well understood, is real estate auction.

Unfortunately, in the context of real estate, most people associate the word 'auction' with unfavorable seller circumstances, such as a foreclosure sale, where the seller has no choice or control. This is because only a relatively small segment of the population has had direct experience with voluntary real estate auctions, where some of the world's most valuable properties are bought and sold. Historically, the overwhelming majority of such auctions have involved commercial properties and high end, luxury homes. But the fact of the matter is that auction is an extremely effective method for maximizing the sale price of residential real estate, and it is available to everyone, not just the rich. Accordingly, we explain when and why sellers should consider this approach.

Of course, marketing is not a seller's sole concern. In a non-auction setting, offers must be negotiated and, ultimately, a sale must be closed. Moreover, throughout the entire selling process many legal requirements must be fulfilled – if they are not, what seems like 'the best deal possible' could turn out to be the worst nightmare imaginable. It is important that the seller be aware of these requirements, especially [but not only] if unrepresented by a real estate broker, and several of the most salient legal issues are discussed in their relevant context.

The content of this book is organized as follows: the first five sections cover marketing – from timing, pricing and advertising to home preparation and presentation, including preliminary inspections and decisions regarding what to repair and what to leave as is, staging, showing, and the auction option. The last two sections cover negotiating and closing a non-auction sale, handling contingencies, and formal closing requirements and procedures. There is an appendix with a sample sales contract and some typical addenda.

Selling a home is a major undertaking, but with the right preparation and guidance it can be a satisfying and economically rewarding one. While this book is intended to help with that preparation, it is not intended as a substitute for the direct guidance of legal and other real estate professionals. It is a fact of life that even the most self-reliant FSBO seller must be prepared to deal with many such professionals, from inspectors and appraisers, brokers and sales agents to title researchers and insurers and the attorneys and legal personnel who handle closings.

The key word here is *professional* – each of these people is an expert in at least one domain and it is unwise, to say the least, for an unprepared lay person to go head-to-head with such an expert, let alone a team of them, especially when the stakes are as high as they are in a real estate transaction. If you are not represented by a broker it is strongly suggested that you cobble together your own cadre of experts that you can call upon for guidance, and one of the purposes of this book is to help you evaluate the capabilities of the local talent.

Here's hoping that your sales experience is an enjoyable and profitable one!

---

# 1. Method of Sale

As noted in the introduction, most people never consider the auction option because they are unfamiliar with the process and associate it with unfavorable circumstances. As a result, relatively little residential real estate is sold voluntarily at auction, and the few properties that are tend to be high-end, luxury homes. This is because the most affluent people are indeed familiar with auction and understand its value well. And while it is not always the best option, quite often it is – often enough that it should be seriously considered by every seller.

Home owners are not the only ones who under-appreciate the auction option. Most residential real estate brokers and salespeople are also unfamiliar with its benefits.

For example, in addition to maximizing selling price and minimizing selling time, auctions usually generate greater broker earnings (that is, as a percentage of selling price). One reason for this is that commissions are paid directly by buyers on top of the sale price. This tends to produce both a larger net to the seller and to the broker. In fact, when a property that has been listed by a broker is sold at auction, the broker can receive the full listing commission plus an auction fee. Again, the fees are paid directly by the buyer, as a distinctly separate cost. And though, in a traditional brokered transaction, buyers are aware that the property price includes a commission, in the heat of the auction atmosphere the fees do not figure into the buying decision in quite the same manner. This is a non-trivial difference: *The market value of real estate, in general, includes commissions, because market value is equal to sales price and the vast majority of home sales are brokered, with the commissions paid at settlement by the seller.*

This is an important fact and should be well understood. Again, most home sales are brokered and involve both a listing and a buying-side commission. That is, the total broker commission typically comprises both a fee to the broker who lists the property and a fee to the broker who brings the buyer – usually two different brokers (although it can be only one, in which case the broker is said to have earned 'both sides' of the deal). Because commissions are virtually always included in the final sale price, the market value of a home includes the average local real estate commission for that market. This is one of the reasons that FSBO sellers usually do not realize market value: Every buyer knows that there is no listing commission (in rare cases there may also be no buying-side commission) and so expect a corresponding discount. In fact, on average, FSBO sellers realize 15% to 20% less[1] than broker-represented sellers, although there are additional reasons for this very high differential (as discussed below).

In addition to choosing the method of sale a seller must also decide how to work with real estate brokers: *Brokers*, plural, because it is extremely unlikely that a sale will be made without the involvement of at least one, *i.e.*, the broker who represents the buyer. And while it is conceivable that a sale will be made to an unrepresented buyer the likelihood of this happening is rather low, almost certainly under 15% and perhaps much lower,[2] depending upon the market. So if a seller is unwilling to work with a broker-represented buyer – or, more accurately, unwilling to pay a commission to a buyer's broker (although commissions are ultimately funded by the buyer it is generally more convenient if it is wrapped into the property price and thence the mortgage), it will probably take an inordinately long time to make a sale. For this reason alone, the only rational question is whether or not to engage a

---

1 FSBOs accounted for 9% of home sales in 2013. The typical FSBO home sold for $184,000 compared to $230,000 for agent-assisted home sales. Source: *The 2014 NAR Profile of Home Buyers and Sellers* (see summary at: http://www.realtor. org/field-guides/field-guide-to-quick-real-estate-statistics).

2 In 2013, 88% of buyers purchased their home through a real estate agent or broker: *Ibid*

listing agent – it should be a foregone conclusion that it is sensible to work with a buyer's agent.[3]

Here there are many factors that should be considered, involving almost every facet of marketing and selling. If a listing broker is engaged, there are multiple types of arrangements that can be made, with varying broker duties and responsibilities (and, of course, fees and splits). The best way to appraise the value of broker representation is to consider these various factors within the context of the selling process, and that is how the topic is addressed here. However, a few fundamental points can be understood in advance of this discussion, simply on the basis of logic.

For example, by asking the question: "If broker representation could be had for free, should it be accepted?" it becomes clear that the only reason *not* to have such rep-

---

3 It should be understood that the terms "broker" and "agent" can refer to the same person/role, but they can also have different meanings. Only a broker can enter directly into an agreement to represent a seller or buyer of real estate (the client). By virtue of such an agreement, the broker becomes an agent of the client. But a broker, in turn, can hire a real estate salesperson to be the broker's representative, who is then an agent of the broker and thereby the client. While both brokers and salespeople must be licensed, the requirements to obtain a broker's license are much greater, as are the responsibilities: The broker is responsible for the actions of the sales people and must supervise their activity. Though sales people are often referred to as agents and are the individuals that clients usually deal with, all agreements that sales people create with clients must be in the name of the broker. In a nutshell, sales people are indirect agents of consumers, and direct agents of brokers. More about these relationships in what follows.

resentation would be if, in some manner, it would make the selling process more difficult and/or less financially rewarding. However, it will become evident in what follows that a competent agent can make an extremely valuable contribution with respect to virtually every aspect of a real estate sale, especially price maximization[4] (and again, because market value always includes commissions, a non-represented seller should expect to receive less than market value – *i.e.*, market value minus the average local commission). Therefore, if seller representation could be had for free, the only reason not to accept it would be on the grounds of agent incompetence.

In light of these facts, a good approach is to look for a reputable real estate auction company that is also a licensed real estate brokerage. If such a company exists in your locale, ask for a free consultation to discuss the auction option. If, based on the estimated market price of your property (see section 3), the auctioneer feels that you can readily meet and likely better that price at auction, you should receive a proposal more or less along the following lines.

1. Your property will be listed in the local MLS at a price intended to stimulate interest (with a comment

---

4 Per reference 1, a competent agent can help the seller realize a sales price that is 15% to 20% higher than that which might be obtained without representation. And so, because the cost of representation is typically only a fraction of this added revenue, it follows that the only real question is: "Can I be sure to obtain competent representation."

that this price is only for the purpose of promoting the auction – more on pricing in the next section).

2. An advertising budget will be proposed and, if accepted, will be paid by you, the seller.[5, 6] (Per the footnote, this is one of the key decision-points regarding the auction option: In general, only sellers who are willing and able to come out-of-pocket for advertising are candidates for auction).

3. The auction date will be set six or seven weeks out, which allows for the holding of two or three open houses.

Of course, it's always possible that you'll receive an offer that will be sufficient to preempt the auction. And it is in any case within your power to set a minimum price that you will accept, though it may make sense to hold an *Absolute* sale (that is, the house will absolutely sell on the day of auction at the highest offered price). While many

---

5 All other costs are borne by the buyer, including commissions and transfer taxes. Because, with brokered sales, taxes are usually shared between the buyer and the seller, this difference alone is generally sufficient to offset the cost of advertising. However, this is a key decision point: Only sellers who are willing and able to come out of pocket for advertising are in a position to choose the auction option.

6 It should be noted that the sort of prominent advertising that is called for with auction is generally *not* cost-effective with a typical, non-auction sale, and brokers *do not*, typically, run such advertising for an individual property – at least not at their own expense, despite what they might lead their prospective clients to believe.

home sellers might consider this to be a bit risky it is quite often the best move, because it produces greater competition (more participants and a more competitive setting). This will be a primary part of the auction proposal and of your discussion with the auctioneer. If you opt for auction, it will be the most crucial decision you must make.

## 2. Timing and Pricing

In accordance with the economics of supply and demand, markets tend to be more advantageous for sellers as the proportion of buyers to sellers increases. A "seller's market" is characterized by an overabundance of buyers in relation to the number of homes for sale. While overall market conditions are not subject to control there are predictable seasonal changes that can be taken advantage of. Generally speaking, buying activity is low between Thanksgiving and New Years and then gradually picks up through January and February, reaching the first of two annual peaks around the beginning of March. Activity more or less remains at this [first peak] level until Memorial Day, then declines and remains relatively low throughout the summer. There is a second peak that begins around Labor Day. It is usually somewhat lower than the first and lasts until a week or two before Thanksgiving.

Homes receive the most attention when they are new to the market – the number of showings tends to decline the longer a property has been for sale. Therefore, if circumstances permit, sellers should aim to begin marketing in the early days of one of the two annual peaks, preferably the first. If a property does not sell during one of these peak periods it is generally best – again, circumstances permitting – to withdraw it from the market until the next peak comes around. It is also crucial to set an appropriate price, because over-priced properties get very few showings (as do 'stale' properties that have been on the market for a prolonged period, which in some markets can be as little as a few weeks). Because of this, overpricing is one of the worst mistakes a seller can make. Nothing creates stale listings more consistently than overpricing.

Determining an optimal offering price requires patience, discipline and research. Most people tend to believe that it is best to start with a price that is a little high, so that they will have "room to negotiate." This strategy ignores the fact that negotiating power is directly proportional to the number of interested buyers who are ready, willing and able to make an offer. Competition among buyers gives sellers the best sort of leverage, and an easy way to stimulate competition is by setting an offering price that is perceived to be less than what the property is worth. Remember: A seller is not obligated to accept an offer just because it is made at the advertised asking price – holding out for a better deal is perfectly legitimate (and, when there are multiple eager buyers, makes good sense). The trick is to come up with an offering price that is close to market value but is perceived as a bargain under current market conditions. Determining this number is one of the most crucial marketing decisions a seller can make, and is addressed in the following section. However, before jumping in there is a little technical detail regarding pricing that merits consideration.

Most buyers have a price range in mind when they begin their property search. Whether they are shopping themselves or an agent is looking for them, a computerized search will almost certainly be conducted – a search that will be delimited by price range: *e.g.*, "houses with features x,y and z under $300,000." Consequently, one way of creating the perception of a bargain is by rounding the offering price down to just below the nearest "round number." For example, if a determination is made that the market value of a house is $304,000 it might make sense to list at $299,000 and thereby cast a wider net – those searching in the under $300,000 range might otherwise miss the offer altogether.

---

# 3. Pre-Listing Inspections and Appraisals

In order to determine an appropriate offering price one must first know what a property is actually worth. There are two primary pieces of information needed for this, *viz*: (1) the condition of the property, and (2) the value and condition of similarly configured and situated properties – *i.e.*, the prices at which such properties have very recently sold in the same market.

The best way to determine property condition is with the help of a professional property inspector. On the other hand, the best way to determine market value is not necessarily with the help of a professional appraiser but rather with a real estate salesperson who knows the market. A formal appraisal can provide helpful information (more on this below) but typically costs several hundred dollars. Moreover, it is generally *not* a better indicator of market value than a Comparable Market Analysis (CMA) from a competent real estate salesperson who knows the market (and CMAs can be had for free, more on this below as well).

Appraisers are not directly familiar with as many comparable properties as an active real estate salesperson, nor are they as familiar with the nuances of the local market. For example, an appraiser is unlikely to know the exact condition of comparable properties ("comps"), at least not by firsthand experience, whereas an active real estate agent will have a good handle on this. In other words, an appraiser is not in as good a position as an active agent to evaluate just how "comparable" the comps are. In fact, appraisers will often seek out the opinion of a local agent or broker to get a handle on some of these factors. Therefore, whether you engage a listing broker or not you should obtain a free CMA from one or more real estate salespeople. (If you are unsure about an agent's competence, you should ask for CMAs from two or three competing agents: This exercise will help you to determine both the value of your home and that of the agent as well.)

As mentioned, a CMA will furnish a comparison of your home to similar properties in two general categories: (1) homes in your neighborhood that have recently sold (preferably in the past several weeks but no more than 6 months ago), and (2) homes in your neighborhood that are currently for sale. It will compare these properties on the basis of their features and condition, including home and lot size, number of rooms by type (bedrooms, bathrooms, etc.), parking and other features of interest. Based on the selling and asking prices of these comps, the real estate agent who prepares the report will estimate the price at which your property will likely sell (of course, a judgement must be made regarding how realistic these asking prices are). The price at which a property sells is deemed its "Fair Market Value," with the presumption that the sale is voluntary and the property was adequately exposed to potential buyers.

A good agent can zero-in very closely on the price your property will sell for, and the quality of a CMA is an indicator of just how competent the agent who produced it is. When evaluating a CMA/agent, your first concern should be to determine just how comparable the comps are. The best way to accomplish this is to visit the currently-for-sale homes that were selected and see for yourself how they stack up to yours (this will also help sharpen your sense of local home values).

Below is a sample CMA, with only three comps in each category for clarity (an actual CMA could include more, and *should* include every close comparable available). You'll notice that it expresses home prices in terms of dollars per square foot (of living space) in order to facilitate comparisons between homes of different sizes. This makes it easy to notice any anomalies – gross over- or underpricing.

As discussed, the report is broken into 2 sections, "Recent Sales" and "Currently on the Market." Actual sale prices, of course, carry the most weight but it is possible to recognize market trends from current asking prices (*i.e.*, the extent to which the market may have risen or fallen since nearby homes were sold).

**RECENT SALES**

| | Data | Subject Property | Comp 1 | Comp 2 | Comp 3 | Data Values | |
|---|---|---|---|---|---|---|---|
| 1 | Address | 1234 Main St | 5678 1st Ave | 9012 2nd St | 345 3rd St | n/a | |
| 2 | Lot Size | 23000 | 15000 | 23750 | 18955 | $ 65,000.00 | /acre |
| 3 | Bedrooms | 3 | 2 | 3 | 2 | $ 25,000.00 | /BR |
| 4 | Baths | 2.5 | 1.5 | 2.0 | 2.5 | $ 15,000.00 | /BA |
| 5 | Garage Spaces | 1 | 2 | 1 | 0 | $ 15,000.00 | /space |
| 6 | Sq Footage | 1900 | 1850 | 1925 | 1950 | n/a | |
| 7 | Sold Price | n/a | $ 155,500.00 | $ 188,500.00 | $ 157,700.00 | n/a | |
| 8 | Sold/sq ft | n/a | $84.05 | $97.92 | $80.87 | n/a | |
| 9 | Adj Lot Size | n/a | $ 11,937.56 | $ (1,119.15) | $ 6,035.93 | n/a | |
| 10 | Adj Bedrooms | n/a | $ 25,000.00 | $ - | $ 25,000.00 | n/a | |
| 11 | Adj Baths | n/a | $ 15,000.00 | $ 7,500.00 | $ - | n/a | |
| 12 | Adj Garage(s) | n/a | $ (15,000.00) | $ - | $ 15,000.00 | n/a | |
| 13 | Adj Sold price | n/a | $ 192,437.56 | $ 194,880.85 | $ 203,735.93 | n/a | |
| 14 | Adj sold/sq ft | n/a | $104.02 | $101.24 | $104.48 | n/a | |
| 15 | Average/sq ft | $103.25 | | | | | |
| | Subject Value | $196,167 | | | | | |

**CURRENTLY ON THE MARKET**

| | Data | Subject Property | Comp 1 | Comp 2 | Comp 3 | Data Values | |
|---|---|---|---|---|---|---|---|
| 1 | Address | 1234 Main St | 568 1st Pl | 912 2nd Ave | 34 3rd Way | n/a | |
| 2 | Lot Size | 23000 | 16500 | 22500 | 21200 | $ 65,000.00 | /acre |
| 3 | Bedrooms | 3 | 2 | 3 | 2 | $ 25,000.00 | /BR |
| 4 | Baths | 2.5 | 2.5 | 3.0 | 2.0 | $ 15,000.00 | /BA |
| 5 | Garage Spaces | 1 | 2 | 2 | 0 | $ 15,000.00 | /space |
| 6 | Sq Footage | 1900 | 1750 | 1825 | 1600 | n/a | |
| 7 | Ask Price | n/a | $ 155,500.00 | $ 188,500.00 | $ 157,700.00 | n/a | |
| 8 | Ask/sq ft | n/a | $88.86 | $103.29 | $98.56 | n/a | |
| 9 | Adj Lot Size | n/a | $ 9,699.27 | $ 746.10 | $ 2,685.95 | n/a | |
| 10 | Adj Bedrooms | n/a | $ 25,000.00 | $ - | $ 25,000.00 | n/a | |
| 11 | Adj Baths | n/a | $ - | $ (7,500.00) | $ 7,500.00 | n/a | |
| 12 | Adj Garage(s) | n/a | $ (15,000.00) | $ (15,000.00) | $ 15,000.00 | n/a | |
| 13 | Adj Ask price | n/a | $ 175,199.27 | $ 166,746.10 | $ 207,885.95 | n/a | |
| 14 | Adj Ask/sq ft | n/a | $100.11 | $91.37 | $129.93 | n/a | |
| 15 | Average/sq ft | $107.14 | | | | | |
| | Subject Value | $203,560 | | | | | |

The sample CMA indicates that $103.25 per square foot would have been the likely Fair Market Value of the subject property 6 months ago, or whenever the closest comparables actually sold. This is determined by finding the comps that are closest in configuration and condition to the subject property and then making allowances for any differences. The right-most column, F – rows two through five – lists the values for the individual data points on which the homes are compared (in this case lot size, bedroom, bathroom and garage parking spaces). In rows nine through thirteen an adjustment is made to each of the home selling prices by comparing these data points to those of the subject property. For example, in row twelve of Comp-1, $15,000 is subtracted from the sale price because it has one more garage space than the subject property. Row thirteen shows the adjusted sale price for each comp and row fourteen the adjusted price per square foot of living space. The average price per square foot of all three comps is $103.25, which gives a value of $196,167 for the subject property ($103.25 per square foot times 1900 square feet).

Determining how the price-per-square-foot may have changed in the interim is what the currently-for-sale comps are for. An estimate of current value is determined by looking for the closest comparables currently for sale, making the same adjustments as for the closest sold comparables, and then judging whether the asking prices are reasonable. From the *Currently on the Market* chart, we see that the average asking price per square foot has increased to $107.14. However, this reflects asking prices, and must be taken with extreme caution.

Here are some things to keep in mind. First, make sure that as many comps as can be found are included in the report. This means every for-sale and sold home in the same neighborhood during the last 6 months. If there aren't any comps within this time frame it will be difficult to estimate current value (this will also be true if there have been major changes in the local economy in the past 6 months). Similarly, if there aren't any comps in the same neighborhood, or very few, it will be necessary to find a "similar" neighborhood or neighborhoods. This is a tricky business, because it involves making judgements not only about different houses but also different locations. There may even be significant differences between different parts of the same neighborhood, just as there may be significant differences in property condition and configuration (again, it is important to make a personal inspection of for-sale comps to form a solid judgement about this). Also, it's possible that the sale or asking price of a comp isn't accurate because of seller concessions.

Finally, you may receive an inflated estimate of your home's value from a real estate agent who is hoping to acquire your business by inflating your hopes. The tactic is simple: Try to convince a potential client that competing agents are purposefully under-estimating the property's value in order to facilitate an easy and quick sale. All of these factors require careful attention and, in the end, subjective judgment. If after evaluating one or more CMAs you feel you have not received objective advice you might finally consider engaging the services of a professional appraiser, but for the reasons discussed this should usually be a last ditch move.

# 4. Property Preparation and Presentation

## Inspections and Inspectors

The best way to evaluate your property's condition is to have a professional inspection done. This won't preclude your buyers from having their own inspection performed but it will provide you with crucial information; information that you need to both properly establish value and prepare for negotiations. It is highly probably that an inspection will uncover multiple issues that you are unaware of, some of which may have a major impact on the value of your home. You will be bargaining from a position of weakness if your buyer discovers these problems before you do.

An incompetent real estate agent may try to persuade you that it is bad selling strategy to have a pre-marketing inspection done. The reasons may seem convincing: if the purchaser wants an inspection they will order their own regardless of the fact that you had one done, so you are wasting money (while it is true that most buyers will want their own inspection this is beside the point). You might also be advised that presenting prospective buyers with bad news early in the sales process is poor salesmanship, and that you don't have to disclose problems that you don't know about.

Knowledge is power. It is much better to be aware of your property's actual value, and therefore its condition, than to believe it has a false, inflated value. As discussed above, improper pricing is one of the worst selling mistakes a home owner can make. Although some pre-sale improvements aren't worth making, because the investment is unlikely to be recouped in the sale price, many are – especially minor ones, and especially when they are connected with routine maintenance issues. This helps with property presentation: Evidence of a well-maintained home goes a long way towards establishing perceived value. If your property does require costly repairs, and if you are unprepared to make them, it is silly to attempt to wrangle buyers who are uninterested in acquiring such a home. Those buyers who are prepared to make repairs will be more than happy to receive a concession to cover them, and your negotiating position will be much stronger if you position the need up-front.

## Repairs, Improvements and Legal Disclosure Requirements

So, just what improvements should you make and which should you avoid? There are no strict rules, but there are some general guidelines. Things that can be done in a short amount of time and are not very costly are no-brainers. By the same logic, large projects are almost always counter-indicated. For example, if you learn from your inspection that your home is in need of a major repair – maybe a new roof or foundation – you must disclose this to potential buyers. But the best way to address this is to get a good handle on the cost of the repair – multiple estimates from reputable contractors – and offer a credit to the buyer for the lowest amount that you believe the work can be done for. This prevents marketing delays, eliminates a large cash outlay (not to mention any liability you may have for the work) and offers the buyer more choice and control (*i.e.*, with respect to when/how/by whom to have the work done).

This last point is especially poignant when it comes to remodeling work. There's no sense making a large cash outlay for a nicer bathroom or kitchen when you have no clue as to the aesthetic preferences of your potential buyers. It makes more sense to make a price concession or offer a credit, so the buyer can decide what to do.

On the other hand, many repairs and aesthetic improvements do make sense. As mentioned, anything related to routine maintenance – e.g., dirty gutters or filters, leaking faucets – are no-brainers, because they give the impression that you do not maintain the property. All inexpensive, non-time-consuming repairs should be made. One can get a good sense of things to look for from the legal disclosure requirements imposed on sellers.

There are federal, state and local government laws regarding the disclosure of property defects and certain other information by home sellers, and it is the responsibility of owners and agents to abide by them. It should be noted that unrepresented, FSBO sellers have the same legal responsibilities as those represented by a broker – all sellers can be held liable, civilly and criminally, by both buyers and governments for infractions of these laws.

In the Appendix are some sample disclosure and disclaimer forms for Maryland.

Again, requirements vary by municipality and state but, in general, sellers must disclose any material fact – *i.e.*, any information that materially affects property value or desirability. Here are some examples.

a. *Overall Property Condition.* Any defect in any part or system, from the roof and foundation to the plumbing and electrical system, insulation, HVAC and appliances, even external items like the sewer or a nearby sink-hole. To minimize liability, seller's should have their own, pre-sale inspection conducted by a certified inspector and encourage buyers to have their own done as well.

b. *Health, Safety and Environmental Hazards.* There are legal requirements for disclosure of the presence of lead paint, asbestos, formaldehyde, radon, chemical storage (*e.g.,* underground fuel tanks) and soil/water contamination – even risk from external sources such as natural disasters (*e.g.,* floods, earthquakes, hurricanes). In addition, there may be local conservation requirements (water, energy).

c. *Legal Condition.* There are requirements regarding legal issues that impact the property, such as improperly established property lines or property improvements; litigation; title problems; HOA, developer and builder requirements.

d. *External and Intangible Conditions.* A seller can be held liable for giving misleading answers to buyer questions about various aspects of the neighborhood, such as the crime rate and school system, or for failing to disclose the presence of a convicted child molester or the occurrence of a repulsive crime – even rumors that the house is haunted because someone was murdered in it.

And of course it is not permitted to include false or inaccurate information in listings and advertisements. The best way to protect yourself from disclosure-related liability is to be as proactive and honest as possible, to use the proper forms for the state and municipality in which you live and to have the guidance of a real estate broker and/ or attorney. If you are represented by a broker yet unsure about any potential legal liability seek the advice of a local real estate attorney.

## Staging and Presentation

Beyond maintenance and repair there are many relatively low-cost, easy to make aesthetic changes that will have a major impact on how a home "shows," both inside and out. Unfortunately, most people either underestimate the importance of this preparation or do not understand how to do it effectively. After the issue of pricing, this is where home owners seem to have the most difficulty forming an objective judgement. And as with improper pricing, improper home preparation delays the sales process and reduces the likelihood of getting top dollar.

This, of course, is why there are professional *stagers* who, like decorators, get paid to create visually appealing home environments – but optimized for marketing, not for being lived-in. However, just as a good real estate agent can furnish a free estimate of value that rivals that of a professional appraisal, so too can a good agent furnish all the [free] advice you need to optimize the presentation of your home. Whether or not you intend to hire a real estate broker to represent you, you should afford yourself the benefit of one or more professional opinions regarding the appearance and preparation of your home for sale.

## Exterior

The old expression "curb appeal" refers to the first impression people receive of a home from its exterior, as they pass by or approach it. While an unkempt lawn or cluttered patio does not have a material effect on the actual market value of a home, such things definitely have an unfavorable emotional effect on prospective buyers. It's counterproductive, to say the least, to discourage prospective purchasers from entering your home.

Broadly speaking, there are two concerns; your house and its surroundings. Items of concern in the surroundings are the lawn, sidewalks, driveway and shrubbery. A nicely landscaped property creates a very positive impression and is well worth the investment of time and/or money. If there are defects in the sidewalks and driveway you should seriously consider repairing them. With respect to the house, it should be freshly painted in a conservative fashion, with colors that fit the neighboring homes. Windows should be kept clean at all times and all aspects of the home exterior should look and function perfectly (all windows and doors should work smoothly, without creaks or squeaks, all gutters should be clean and intact, all lights should function).

By the way, your 'FOR SALE' sign is a crucial exterior feature. Make sure it is in perfect condition, clearly readable and that it contains all crucial information: phone number, email and web address, plus broker info if appropriate, otherwise the 'BY OWNER' designation. A weatherproof container with flyers is helpful and generally expected.

## Interior

As with the exterior, the inside should be freshly painted (conservatively, with light colors, to make spaces appear as large as possible), bright and well-lighted, totally uncluttered (with no visible personal items if possible) and spotlessly clean, with no unpleasant aromas from carpets, drapery, upholstery and especially pets and their accouterments (and preferably some pleasant ones from flowers, potpourri, freshly baked cookies, etc.). Everything should function perfectly, especially sinks and drains. If it's winter and there is a fireplace, keep it lit and the house warm during showings (and cool in summer). Closets and rooms should be as empty as possible, and this applies to furniture. To get a good idea of what to shoot for visit the model homes of some local builders; they use professional stagers to create ideal selling environments. While this entails a good amount of effort, and some expenditures – you'll need a place to store excess furniture and other items – if done properly it will have an enormous impact on the impression your home makes to buyers.

## Showing

As with pricing and preparation, presentation is a misunderstood topic and showings are almost always handled poorly by home owners. Unfortunately, most owners succumb to the misconception that, because they "know their home" better than anybody else, they are best qualified to show it. But as discussed in connection with the subjects of pricing and preparation, it is very difficult for an owner to view their home objectively.

Fortunately, this challenge has an extremely easy solution. In a nutshell, the best thing an owner can do when prospective buyers visit their home is make themselves scarce. Nothing cramps a buyer's style and blunts their interest in a property like the seller's looming presence. Beyond the normal squeamishness people feel about intruding upon the privacy of others and poking around their things (one of the reasons personal artifacts should not be visible) buyers are reluctant to "kick the tires" and ask questions that might cause embarrassment or hostility.

Owners should always strive to be away during showings, which are best conducted by the real estate agent who represents the buyer. The next best option is the seller's agent. If these options aren't available, the best thing an owner can do is simply furnish a little information, offer to answer any questions, and then politely stay out of the way.

# 5. Advertising and Open Houses

Advertising is probably the fourth most misunderstood aspect of home selling. There are a couple of things that work very well, and much that does not. It is easy to understand why this is so if two facts are kept in mind, namely: (1) Most buyers begin their search online and/or find their home through a real estate agent (approximately 90%)[7] and (2) The overwhelming majority of online home listings originate in local multiple listing services, which the most heavily trafficked web sites pull from (e.g., Realtor.com, Zillow.com, major newspapers' online classifieds, etc.). *MLS data goes everywhere*: It is distributed on agent websites, on blogs and social media – everywhere.

For these reasons an MLS listing is, in conjunction with an old-fashioned "FOR SALE" sign, the most powerful advertising available to a typical home seller. It is possible to position a property in some well-trafficked sites without listing it with an MLS (*e.g.*, Zillow has a FSBO category). But because the exposure this provides is only a fraction of that provided by an MLS listing, and because most buyers are represented by a real estate agent (who use the MLS almost exclusively to find properties to show their clients), this is a very weak alternative.

There are some cases where special-purpose advertising can be very helpful, especially in the auction context (as discussed in section 1) and possibly for open houses (more on open houses below). This might include prominent display ads in high circulation print publications

---

and well-trafficked websites, even billboards and possibly radio. But the cost of special exposure has to be justified by the price that the sale is likely to bring – and unless a property is unusual, it isn't likely that such exposure will expedite things enough to justify the expense.

On the other hand, because of the primacy of online searches it is extremely beneficial to have an extensive collection of high-quality, professionally produced photos posted with your listing (and, in some cases, a professionally produced video tour – as is the case with special advertising, this makes sense when the property price justifies the expense, or when the property has unusual features that can be shown to advantage in this format).

A word on Open Houses: While you might not hear this elsewhere, don't expect too much from them (or from Broker Opens, where agents from local brokerages are invited, usually by mass-email, to an agent-only open house, for free lunch and a tour of the property). Open Houses can be helpful – again, they are especially important for auctions – but the vast majority of sales originate with an MLS listing and the good-old yard sign.

And a word for FSBO sellers: There are special challenges that FSBO sellers face. As noted, buyer's agents use their local MLS when selecting properties to show their clients. And some agents may be reluctant to show FSBO properties. For example, they might expect to have difficulties dealing directly with an owner, and so feel that they will be doing the work of two agents. Moreover, buyers – and certainly their agents – know that with a FSBO there is no listing commission, and so expect a discount  to reflect that fact. Unrepresented buyers can be even more problematic – they often target FSBOs for special concessions, such as seller-financing, with the expectation that unrepresented sellers are vulnerable to exploitation. Because of this, FSBOs tend to encounter more than their fair share of unqualified and even fraudulent buyers.

---

# 6. Negotiations and Contingencies

Negotiating a home sale is a fairly complex matter and gives non-business people a chance to experience something they would probably never otherwise encounter. American consumers are generally unaccustomed to bargaining over price, but when they sometimes do – perhaps when buying a car – the negotiating points involved are relatively limited. Buying or selling a house, on the other hand, is much more like a business deal than a consumer transaction. There are many complex variables and legal issues involved, which vary by state and municipality. This is why real estate brokers are limited to the use of standardized forms (forms that have been vetted by the local real estate board and its attorneys – only an attorney who specializes in real estate law should write agreements from scratch or make changes to the language used in a standard contract).

The Appendix contains a sample sales contract for Maryland, including frequently used notices and addenda. Each blank space represents a negotiating point. A glance at this form should make it clear that there is no substitute for the advice of a real estate attorney or other real estate professional. On the other hand, there is one bit of general guidance that can be offered with confidence.

People without business experience may have difficulty accommodating themselves to the fact that emotions can not be allowed to cloud negotiations. In the discussions of pricing, preparation, and presentation, the crucial role of objectivity was stressed, and it is of especial importance here. Negotiations can quickly become "heated," and the party with the least objectivity and control over their emotions bargains from a disadvantaged position. This is one of the reasons a seller's agent is generally able to negotiate better terms than a seller: aside from the fact that agents are professional negotiators they are also not principals in the transaction and, perhaps most crucially, do not have a personal tie to the property. They are therefore able to view things from a somewhat more objective perspective.

As you can see from the sample documents, the number of variables and open matters subject to negotiation is substantial, so it is not practicable to offer detailed advice in advance. And while there are many logical, more-or-less accepted tactics for dealing with various negotiating situations – *e.g.*, how to handle multiple offers – there is no fixed, "right" answer for every circumstance. However, a few guidelines regarding contingencies and the offer/counter-offer procedure are in order.

Because there is no sale until contingencies are fulfilled it is paramount for sellers not only to follow through with their own obligations but to monitor the buyer's progress as well. At the very least, most purchase offers are contingent upon the buyer securing a loan and conducting a property inspection, and it is usually agreed that unless these contingencies are eliminated in a manner that satisfies the buyer, the buyer can walk away from the deal without forfeiting the Earnest Money Deposit (the "good faith" money that buyers submit with an offer to purchase, which is held in trust by a third party – usually the seller's real estate broker, at least until Escrow).

In general – *i.e.*, given market conditions that are not unusual – sellers must agree to contingencies such as these if they wish to receive a fair market price in a reasonable time frame. However, some buyers may try to "tie a seller up" without a firm commitment of their own, and this can be done with buyer-side contingencies. The best way for a seller to avoid this is with some due diligence regarding the buyer's circumstances. For example, unless the buyer can produce evidence that a loan is likely to be obtained it is not advisable to allow a finance contingency. Most buyers will provide a pre-approval letter from a lender, which means that they have passed a fairly in-depth credit analysis. But lenders will also furnish a "pre-qualification" letter, which only means that, based on incomplete and unverified information that the buyer has provided, the lender has furnished an opinion as to what sort of loan can be obtained.

It is also important to understand a bit of contract law, especially the legal issues surrounding offers and counter-offers. The one contingency that a seller can always count on is that a time limit will be placed on a buyer's offer to purchase. This is necessary to prevent the buyer from being tied-up indefinitely, and to prevent the seller from "shopping" the offer (using the fact that there is a "bird in hand" to solicit better offers from other prospects). If the seller does not accept the offer before the time limit expires, or counters with a different proposal, the original offer becomes null and void – and if the seller's counter offer is not accepted then it, too, is nullified.

Each counter proposal is a new, legal offer, which nullifies the previous one and only becomes a binding agreement if it is accepted as proposed, in accordance with any stipulations it might contain, such as a time limit. Illustratively, if a seller makes a counter to a buyer's offer, and the buyer rejects it, the seller no longer has the unilateral right to accept the original offer – that is, to create a binding agreement by accepting it (of course, if the buyer agrees, the original offer can be revived and become the basis for a contract).

One final note on the subject of negotiations: it is often taken for granted that there is a "going rate" for the services of the various professionals involved in a real estate transaction, especially agent services. But broker commissions are and must always be negotiable – by law. When evaluating a prospective real estate salesperson, ask about the agent's fees and how he/she justifies them. In most cases the commission is set by the brokerage and the agent receives only a fraction of what is charged, especially new, inexperienced agents. However, a competent agent will have control over their rates and should be able to justify them to the seller.

# 7. Closing the Deal

## Procedures and Verifications

While it is conceivable that a buyer and seller might reach a ratified agreement without the moderation of any third parties – *e.g.*, without the involvement of a buyer's or a seller's broker, a real estate attorney, etc. – when it comes to settlement this isolation must end. Even if, for some inexplicable reason, no one has ordered an inspection, an appraisal or a title search (which is only conceivable in an all cash deal), there must be a neutral third party to handle the transfer of title and funds.

However, before delving into the mechanics of closing, a few words on the neutrality of third parties is in order. The above-described scenario – a deal getting to closing without the involvement of a single real estate professional – is conceivable but quite unlikely. A somewhat more probable scenario is one in which a broker-represented buyer purchases a house from a FSBO seller, in which case the deal is moderated by a third party but the moderator is not neutral with respect to the interests of the principals. It is important for unrepresented sellers to understand just how far the responsibilities of a buyer's broker extend with respect to the seller's interests.

A real estate agent owes a special, fiduciary duty to a client: Agents must champion clients' interests above all others' – *including their own*. When dealing with a seller on behalf of the buyer, the agent is obligated to maximize the buyer's advantage. Of course, the agent cannot treat the seller dishonestly, but this does not make for neutrality.

For example, if the agent knows that the maximum price the buyer is willing to pay for a property is higher than the asking price, this information must be kept confidential. On the other hand, if the agent somehow overhears that the seller will accept less than the asking price, that information will necessarily be shared with the buyer. Confidentiality, as with other fiduciary responsibilities, is a duty that is owed only to clients. Accordingly, a single agent cannot represent both parties to a transaction.[8]

That being said, here are some of the things a seller should be prepared for regarding settlement. As noted, closings are handled by a neutral third party managing a sort of trust for all the stakeholders in the transaction. This trust is called *Escrow*, a term also used to refer to the items that are held in trust, such as sales contracts and earnest money deposits, and it also used as a verb – as in, "the sales contract has been *escrowed*."

Escrow should be established as soon as an offer is ratified. Practices vary with location, but escrow will likely be administered by a law firm or a title company. Either the seller or the buyer, or an agent of the seller or buyer, "opens escrow" – that is to say, delivers all documents and funds

---

8 A *brokerage* can represent both the buyer and seller but different agents must be assigned to them. This is known as Dual Representation, and both parties must explicitly agree to it in writing. And though a single agent can represent one of the parties to a transaction while providing general information and assistance to the other, *only the represented party is a client of the agent* - the other party is referred to as a *customer*, and this comprises a very different kind of relationship, per the example above.

being held to the *escrow holder* (or *officer* – again, at a law firm or title company). In practice, the escrow holder is usually recommended by one of the real estate agents involved in the transaction. In the scenario discussed above, the buyer's broker would most likely open escrow. Escrow costs vary with property sale price and are allocated to the buyer and seller in accordance with agreement or accepted practice, which also varies by location. These costs range from several hundred to several thousand dollars.

Key functions of the escrow officer are:

a. *Ordering a Title Search.* There are many forms of property ownership, or "estates in land." An estate in land defines the degree, quantity, nature, and extent of an owner's interest in real property. Many types of estates exist, and this is a technical legal subject. Moreover, the type of ownership that is being transferred must be agreed as between the buyer and the seller, so this is crucial information. Suffice it here to say that a title search seeks to establish the extent of the ownership that the seller holds, including all encumbrances and easements – such as liens associated with a loan or judgement, rights to access the property that might be held by neighbors or utilities, etc.

b. *Reporting.* Based on this search, the escrow company will issue a preliminary report describing their findings regarding the seller's title to the property. As seller, it is crucial that you review and thoroughly understand this report – if any detail escapes you, seek help from a relevant professional, either someone at the title company, a real estate agent or your own attorney.

c. *Requesting Payoff.* Any lien on the property should be extinguished at settlement, so that clear title can transfer. The escrow officer obtains payoff instructions from all lien holders – how much to pay to whom at closing.

d. *Preparing Closing Statement.* The closing statement details every aspect of the transaction – credits and debits to the buyer, seller and every other stakeholder associated with the transaction (mortgage company, inspectors, appraisers, etc., including the escrow company itself).

e. *Holding and Disbursing Funds.* The escrow company holds and then disburses all funds at settlement in accordance with the closing statement.

f. *Preparing and Recording Documents.* At settlement, the seller executes a grant deed, which transfers title to the buyer. The escrow officer drafts this deed and records it at closing.

Once escrow is opened, you can contact the escrow officer and ask for an early draft of the closing statement and an estimate of your closing costs, which of course will be subject to change. However, this will establish a point of contact for you at the escrow company and you can keep yourself apprised of how things are progressing. As you near the scheduled settlement date uncertainties should be eliminated and an updated closing statement should give you an accurate picture of your costs.

## 8. Some After Words

As noted in the introduction, this little book is not intended as a comprehensive real estate manual but rather as a helpful guide to the preparation needed to successfully market and sell a home. It cannot be a substitute for the assistance and advice of qualified professionals directly familiar with the reader's circumstances. On the other hand, there is much of value in the pages of this short guide that might not be found elsewhere, including the words of advice of some of the real estate professionals whom the reader may encounter.

For example, it was mentioned in section 3 that an inexperienced or unethical agent might be inclined to give a prospective client selling a home an unrealistically high expectation of the price the home should command. The intended effect is that the seller will believe other, competing agents are under-valuing the property in order to facilitate a quick sale. In other words, every seller needs to have a handle on certain key issues, if for no other reason than to be prepared to evaluate the advice of prospective agents.

The primary issues that we have focused on are: timing, pricing and method of sale; home preparation and presentation; and negotiating/closing. These are not only crucial aspects of a home sale but also the ones that sellers most often tend to misunderstand or handle poorly. And while we have not sought to anticipate every circumstance the seller might encounter we have furnished a solid foundation on which to develop strategies for dealing with each of these primary issues. There is, of course, no substitute for experience. However, by talking to real estate agents and auctioneers, reviewing CMAs, visiting comparables, visiting the model homes of local builders, talking to escrow agents, and to inspectors, and possibly even to appraisers, home sellers can get a pretty good feel for their local market – and how best to approach it.

Again, here's hoping that your home selling experience is an enjoyable and profitable one!

# APPENDIX

# Sales Contract with Disclosures

What follows is a blank residential contract of sale approved by the Maryland Association of Realtors®, including seller disclosures and disclaimers. Please note that this sample contains only the bare essentials of a typical residential real estate transaction, and that an actual agreement may include much more. Accordingly, at the end of this Appendix the reader will find a list of standard MAR forms, which may give an idea of how complex a sale can be.

It should also be noted that the various county and city real estate boards publish their own approved documents, with language specific to the laws of their respective local jurisdictions: In other words, this MAR list comprises what might be thought of as "generic" Maryland forms, while sellers should always try to use those templates that are specific to their county or city.

### RESIDENTIAL CONTRACT OF SALE

*This is a Legally Binding Contract; If Not Understood, Seek Competent Legal Advice.*
**THIS FORM IS DESIGNED AND INTENDED FOR THE SALE AND PURCHASE OF IMPROVED SINGLE FAMILY RESIDENTIAL REAL ESTATE LOCATED IN MARYLAND ONLY.** *FOR OTHER TYPES OF PROPERTY INCLUDE APPROPRIATE ADDENDA.*

**TIME IS OF THE ESSENCE.** Time is of the essence of this Contract. The failure of Seller or Buyer to perform any act as provided in this Contract by a prescribed date or within a prescribed time period shall be a default under this Contract and the non-defaulting party, upon written notice to the defaulting party, may declare this Contract null and void and of no further legal force and effect. In such event, all Deposit(s) shall be disbursed in accordance with Paragraph 19 of this Contract.

**1. DATE OF OFFER:** _____ .

**2. SELLER:** _____

**3. BUYER:** _____

**4. PROPERTY:** Seller does sell to Buyer and Buyer does purchase from Seller, all of the following described Property (hereinafter "Property") known as _____
located in _____ City/County, Maryland, Zip Code _____ ,
together with the improvements thereon, and all rights and appurtenances thereto belonging.

**5. ESTATE:** The Property is being conveyed: _____ in fee simple or _____ subject to an annual ground rent, now existing, in the amount of _____
_____ Dollars ($ _____ ) payable semi-annually, as now or to be recorded among the
Land Records of _____ City/County, Maryland.

**6. PURCHASE PRICE:** The purchase price is _____
_____ Dollars ($ _____ ).

**7. PAYMENT TERMS:** The payment of the purchase price shall be made by Buyer as follows:
(a) An initial Deposit by way of _____ in the amount of _____
_____ Dollars ($ _____ ) at the time of this offer.
(b) An additional Deposit by way of _____ in the amount of _____
_____ Dollars ($ _____ ) to be paid _____
_____ .
(c) All Deposits will be held in escrow by: _____ .
    (If not a Maryland licensed real estate broker, the parties may execute a separate escrow deposit agreement.)
(d) The purchase price less any and all Deposits shall be paid in full by Buyer in cash, wired funds, bank check, certified check or other payment acceptable to the settlement officer at settlement.
(e) Buyer and Seller instruct broker named in paragraph (c) above to place the Deposits in: **(Check One)**
        ☐ A non-interest bearing account;
  **OR** ☐ An interest bearing account, the interest on which, in absence of default by Buyer, shall accrue to the benefit
        of Buyer. Broker may charge a fee for establishing an interest bearing account.

**8. SETTLEMENT:** Date of Settlement _____ or sooner if agreed to in writing by the parties.

**9. FINANCING:** Buyer's obligation to purchase the Property is contingent upon Buyer obtaining a written commitment for a loan secured by the Property as follows **(Check One)**:

☐ Conventional Financing Addendum  ☐ USDA Financing Addendum    ☐ Owner Financing Addendum
☐ FHA Financing Addendum        ☐ Assumption Addendum       ☐ No Financing Contingency
☐ VA Financing Addendum         ☐ Gift of Funds Contingency Addendum  ☐ OTHER:_____

**10. FINANCING APPLICATION AND COMMITMENT:** Buyer agrees to make a written application for the financing as herein described within _____ ( _____ ) days from the Date of Contract Acceptance.

Buyer _____ / _____        Page 1 of 10   10/15        Seller _____ / _____

If a written financing commitment is not obtained by Buyer within _____
( _____ ) days from the Date of Contract Acceptance: (1) Seller, at Seller's election and upon written notice to Buyer, may declare this Contract null and void and of no further legal effect; or (2) Buyer, upon written notice to Seller, which shall include written evidence from the lender of Buyer's inability to obtain financing as provided in Paragraph 9 of this Contract, may declare this Contract null and void and of no further legal effect. In either case, the deposit shall be disbursed in accordance with the Deposit paragraph of this Contract. If Buyer has complied with all of Buyer's obligations under this Contract, including those with respect to applying for financing and seeking to obtain financing, then the Release of Deposit agreement shall provide that the deposit shall be returned to Buyer.

**11. ALTERNATE FINANCING:** Provided Buyer timely and diligently pursues the financing described in Paragraph 9 **"Financing"**; Paragraph 10 **"Financing Application and Commitment"**; and the provisions of Paragraph 28 **"Buyer Responsibility"**, Buyer, at Buyer's election, may also apply for alternate financing. If Buyer, at Buyers sole option, obtains a written commitment for financing in which the loan amount, term of note, amortization period, interest rate, down payment or loan program differ from the financing as described in Paragraph 9, or any addendum to this Contract, the provision of Paragraph 10 or any addendum to this Contract shall be deemed to have been fully satisfied. Such alternate financing may not increase costs to Seller or exceed the time allowed to secure the financing commitment as provided in Paragraph 10, or any addendum to this Contract.

**12. HOME AND/OR ENVIRONMENTAL INSPECTION:** Buyer acknowledges, subject to Seller acceptance, that Buyer is afforded the opportunity, at Buyer's sole cost and expense, to condition Buyer's purchase of the Property upon a Home Inspection and/or Environmental Inspection in order to ascertain the physical condition of the Property or the existence of environmental hazards. If Buyer desires a Home Inspection and/or Environmental Inspection contingency, such contingency must be included in an addendum to this Contract. Buyer and Seller acknowledge that Brokers, agents or subagents are not responsible for the existence or discovery of property defects.

Inspection(s) Addenda Attached _____ _____      Inspection(s) Declined _____ _____
                        Buyer    Buyer                                       Buyer    Buyer

**13. INCLUSIONS/EXCLUSIONS:** Included in the purchase price are all permanently attached fixtures, including all smoke detectors. Certain other **now existing items** which may be considered personal property, whether installed or stored upon the property, are included if box below is checked.

| INCLUDED | INCLUDED | INCLUDED | INCLUDED |
|---|---|---|---|
| ☐ Alarm System | ☐ Exhaust Fan(s) # _____ | ☐ Pool, Equipment & Cover | ☐ Trash Compactor |
| ☐ Built-in Microwave | ☐ Exist. W/W Carpet | ☐ Refrigerator(s) # _____ | ☐ Wall Oven(s) # _____ |
| ☐ Ceiling Fan(s) # _____ | ☐ Fireplace Screen Doors | ☐ w/ice maker | ☐ Water Filter |
| ☐ Central Vacuum | ☐ Freezer | ☐ Satellite Dish | ☐ Water Softener |
| ☐ Clothes Dryer | ☐ Furnace Humidifier | ☐ Screens | ☐ Window A/C Unit(s) |
| ☐ Clothes Washer | ☐ Garage Opener(s) # _____ | ☐ Shades/Blinds | # _____ |
| ☐ Cooktop | w/remote(s) # _____ | ☐ Storage Shed(s) # _____ | ☐ Window Fan(s) # _____ |
| ☐ Dishwasher | ☐ Garbage Disposer | ☐ Storm Doors | ☐ Wood Stove |
| ☐ Drapery/Curtain Rods | ☐ Hot Tub, Equipment & Cover | ☐ Storm Windows | |
| ☐ Draperies/Curtains | ☐ Intercom | ☐ Stove or Range | |
| ☐ Electronic Air Filter | ☐ Playground Equipment | ☐ T.V. Antenna | |

ADDITIONAL INCLUSIONS (SPECIFY): _____

ADDITIONAL EXCLUSIONS (SPECIFY): _____

**14. AGRICULTURALLY ASSESSED PROPERTY:** The Property, or any portion thereof, may be subject to an Agricultural Land Transfer Tax as imposed by Section 13-301 et seq. of the Tax-Property Article, Annotated Code of Maryland, by reason of the Property's having been assessed on the basis of agricultural use. Agricultural taxes assessed as a result of this transfer shall be paid by _____ .

**15. FOREST CONSERVATION AND MANAGEMENT PROGRAM:** Buyer is hereby notified that this transfer may be subject to the Forest Conservation and Management Program imposed by Section 8-211 of the Tax-Property Article, Annotated Code of Maryland. Forest Conservation and Management program taxes assessed as a result of this transfer shall be paid by _____ .

**16. LEAD-BASED PAINT:**
**A. FEDERAL LEAD-BASED PAINT LAW:** Title X, Section 1018, the Residential Lead-Based Paint Hazard Reduction Act of 1992 (the "Act"), requires the disclosure by Seller of information regarding lead-based paint and lead-based paint hazards in connection with the sale of any **residential** real property on which a residential dwelling was constructed prior to 1978. Unless otherwise exempt by the Act, the disclosure shall be made on the required federal Disclosure of Information on Lead-Based Paint and/or Lead-Based Paint Hazards form. **Seller and any agent involved in the transaction are required to retain a copy of the completed Lead-Based Paint Disclosure form for a period of three (3) years following the date of settlement. A Seller who fails to give the required Lead-Based Paint Disclosure form and EPA pamphlet may be liable under the Act for three times the amount of damages and may be subject to both civil and criminal penalties.**

Buyer acknowledges by Buyer's initials below that Buyer has read and understands the provisions of Paragraph 16.A.

_____ / _____ **(BUYER)**

**B. RENOVATION, REPAIR AND PAINTING OF PROPERTY:** In accordance with the Lead Renovation, Repair and Painting Rule ("RRP") as adopted by the Environmental Protection Agency ("the EPA"), effective April 22, 2010, if the improvements on the Property were built before 1978, contractor(s) engaged by Seller to renovate, repair or paint the Property must be certified by the EPA where such work will disturb more than six square feet of paint per room for interior projects; more than 20 square feet of paint for any exterior project; or includes window replacement or demolition ("Covered Work"). Before and during any Covered Work project, contractor(s) must comply with all requirements of the RRP.

A Seller who personally performs any Covered Work on a rental property is required to be certified by the EPA prior to performing such Covered Work. No certification is required for a Seller who personally performs Covered Work on the Seller's principal residence. However, Seller has the ultimate responsibility for the safety of Seller's family or children while performing such Covered Work. For detailed information regarding the RRP, Seller should visit http://www2.epa.gov/lead/renovation-repair-and-painting-program.

Buyer acknowledges by Buyer's initials below that Buyer has read and understands Paragraph 16.B.

_____ / _____ **(BUYER)**

**C. MARYLAND LEAD POISONING PREVENTION PROGRAM:** Under the Maryland Lead Poisoning Prevention Program (the "Maryland Program"), any residential dwelling constructed prior to 1978 that is leased for residential purposes is required to be registered with the Maryland Department of the Environment (MDE). If the Property was built prior to 1978 and is now or has been a rental property or may become a rental property in the future, a separate Maryland Lead-Based Paint Disclosure form is attached. Detailed information regarding compliance requirements may be obtained at: http://www.mde.state.md.us/programs/Land/LeadPoisoningPrevention/Pages/index.aspx.

Buyer acknowledges by Buyer's initials below that Buyer has read and understands Paragraph 16.C.

_____ / _____ **(BUYER)**

**17. ADDENDA/DISCLOSURES:** The Addenda checked below, which are hereby attached, are made a part of this Contract:

- ☐ Affiliated Business Disclosure Notice
- ☐ As Is
- ☐ Cash Appraisal Contingency
- ☐ Condominium Resale Notice
- ☐ Conservation Easement
- ☐ Disclosure of Licensee Status
- ☐ Federal Lead-Based Paint and Lead-Based Hazards Disclosure of Information
- ☐ First-Time Maryland Home Buyer Transfer & Recordation Tax
- ☐ Homeowners Association Notice
- ☐ Kickout
- ☐ Local City/County Certifications/Registrations
- ☐ Local City/County Notices/Disclosure

- ☐ Maryland Lead Poisoning Prevention Program Disclosure
- ☐ MD Non-Resident Seller Transfer Withholding Tax
- ☐ Notice to Buyer and Seller – Maryland Residential Real Property Disclosure/Disclaimer Act
- ☐ On-Site Sewage Disposal System Inspection
- ☐ Property Inspections
- ☐ Property Subject to Ground Rent
- ☐ Purchase Price Escalation
- ☐ Sale, Financing, Settlement or Lease of Other Real Estate
- ☐ Seller Contribution
- ☐ Seller's Purchase of Another Property
- ☐ Short Sale
- ☐ Third Party Approval
- ☐ Water Quality

☐ Other Addenda/Special Conditions:

_____
_____.

**18. WOOD DESTROYING INSECT INSPECTION:** Buyer, at Buyer's expense, (if VA, then at Seller's expense) is authorized to obtain a written report on the state regulated form from a Maryland licensed pest control company that, based on a careful visual inspection, there is no evidence of termite or other wood-destroying insect infestation in the residence or within three (3) feet of the residence; and damage due to previous infestation has been repaired. The provisions of this paragraph also shall apply to: (1) the garage or within three (3) feet of the garage (whether attached or detached); (2) any outbuildings located within three feet of the residence or garage; and (3) a maximum of ten (10) linear feet of the nearest portion of a fence on Seller's Property within three (3) feet of the residence or garage. If there is evidence of present infestation as described above, or if damage caused by present or prior infestation is discovered, Seller, at Seller's expense, shall repair any damage caused by present or prior infestation and have the present infestation treated by a licensed pest control company. If the cost of treatment and repair of such damage exceeds 2% of the purchase price, Seller may, at Seller's option, cancel this Contract, unless Buyer, at Buyer's option should choose to pay for the cost of treatment and repairs exceeding 2% of the purchase price, then this Contract shall remain in full force and effect. If such report reveals damage for which the cost of treatment and repair exceeds 2% of the purchase price, Seller's decision regarding treatment and repair of damage shall be communicated in writing to Buyer within five (5) days from receipt of the report, after which Buyer shall respond to Seller in writing with Buyer's decision within three (3) days from receipt of Seller's notification of Seller's decision. If Seller does not notify Buyer in writing of Seller's decision within five (5) days from receipt of report, Buyer may, at Buyer's option, pay for the cost of treatment and repairs exceeding 2% of the purchase price. If Buyer does not want to pay for the cost of treatment and repairs exceeding 2% of the purchase price, Buyer may terminate this Contract upon written notice delivered to Seller. In the event this Contract is terminated under the terms of this paragraph, the Deposit(s) shall be disbursed in accordance with the Deposit paragraph of this Contract.

**19. DEPOSIT:** If the Deposit is held by a Broker as specified in Paragraph 7(c) of this Contract, Buyer hereby authorizes and directs Broker to hold the Deposit instrument without negotiation or deposit until the parties have executed and accepted this Contract. Upon acceptance, the initial Deposit and additional Deposits (the "Deposit"), if any, shall be placed in escrow as provided in Paragraph 7(e) of this Contract and in accordance with the requirements of Section 17-502(b)(1) of the Business Occupations and Professions Article, Annotated Code of Maryland. If Seller does not execute and accept this Contract, the initial Deposit instrument shall be promptly returned to Buyer. The Deposit shall be disbursed at settlement. In the event this Contract shall be terminated or settlement does not occur, Buyer and Seller agree that the Deposit shall be disbursed by Broker only in accordance with a Release of Deposit agreement executed by Buyer and Seller. In the event Buyer and/or Seller fail to complete the real estate transaction in accordance with the terms and conditions of this Contract, and either Buyer or Seller shall be unable or unwilling to execute a Release of Deposit agreement, Buyer and Seller hereby acknowledge and agree that Broker may distribute the Deposit in accordance with the provisions of Section 17-505(b) of the Business Occupations and Professions Article, Annotated Code of Maryland.

**20. DEED AND TITLE:** Upon payment of the purchase price, a deed for the Property containing covenants of special warranty and further assurances (except in the case of transfer by personal representative of an estate), shall be executed by Seller and shall convey the Property to Buyer. Title to the Property, including all chattels included in the purchase, shall be good and merchantable, free of liens and encumbrances except as specified herein; except for use and occupancy restrictions of public record which are generally applicable to properties in the immediate neighborhood or the subdivision in which the Property is located and publicly recorded easements for public utilities and any other easements which may be observed by an inspection of the Property. Buyer expressly assumes the risk that restrictive covenants, zoning laws or other recorded documents may restrict or prohibit the use of the Property for the purpose(s) intended by Buyer. In the event Seller is unable to give good and merchantable title or such as can be insured by a Maryland licensed title insurer, with Buyer paying not more than the standard rate as filed with the Maryland Insurance Commissioner, Seller, at Seller's expense, shall have the option of curing any defect so as to enable Seller to give good and merchantable title or, if Buyer is willing to accept title without said defect being cured, paying any special premium on behalf of Buyer to obtain title insurance on the Property to the benefit of Buyer. In the event Seller elects to cure any defects in title, this Contract shall continue to remain in full force and effect; and the date of settlement shall be extended for a period not to exceed fourteen (14) additional days. If Seller is unable to cure such title defect(s) and is unable to obtain a policy of title insurance on the Property to the benefit of Buyer from a Maryland licensed title insurer, Buyer shall have the option of taking such title as Seller can give, or terminating this Contract and being reimbursed by Seller for cost of searching title as may have been incurred not to exceed 1/2 of 1% of the purchase price. In the latter event, there shall be no further liability or obligation on either of the parties hereto; and this Contract shall become null and void; and all Deposit(s) shall be disbursed in accordance with the Deposit paragraph of this Contract. In no event shall Broker(s) or their agent(s) have any liability for any defect in Seller's title.

**21. CONDITION OF PROPERTY AND POSSESSION:** At settlement, Seller shall deliver possession of the Property and shall deliver the Property vacant, clear of trash and debris, broom clean and in substantially the same condition as existed on the Date of Contract Acceptance. Buyer reserves the right to inspect the Property within five (5) days prior to settlement. **EXCEPT AS OTHERWISE SPECIFIED IN THIS CONTRACT, INCLUDING THIS PARAGRAPH, THE PROPERTY IS SOLD "AS IS."** The obligations of Seller as provided in this paragraph shall be in addition to any Disclosure and Disclaimer Statement as required by Section 10-702, Real Property Article, Annotated Code of Maryland and any provision of any inspection contingency addendum made a part of this Contract (See Property Inspections Notice).

**22. ADJUSTMENTS:** Ground rent, homeowner's association fees, rent and water rent shall be adjusted and apportioned as of date of settlement; and all taxes, general or special, and all other public or governmental charges or assessments against the Property which are or may be payable on a periodic basis, including Metropolitan District Sanitary Commission, Washington Suburban Sanitary Commission, or other benefit charges, assessments, liens or encumbrances for sewer, water, drainage, paving, or other public improvements completed or commenced on or prior to the date hereof, or subsequent thereto, are to be adjusted and apportioned as of the date of settlement and are to be assumed and paid thereafter by Buyer, whether assessments have been levied or not as of date of settlement if applicable by local law. Any heating or cooking fuels remaining in supply tank(s) at time of settlement shall become the property of Buyer.

**23. SETTLEMENT COSTS:** Buyer agrees to pay all settlement costs and charges including, but not limited to, all Lender's fees in connection herewith, including title examination and title insurance fees, loan insurance premiums, all document preparation and recording fees, notary fees, survey fees where required, and all recording charges, except those incident to clearing existing encumbrances or title defects, except if Buyer is a Veteran obtaining VA financing, those prohibited to be paid by a Veteran obtaining VA financing, which prohibited charges shall be paid by Seller.

**24. TRANSFER CHARGES:**
    **A. IN GENERAL.** Section 14-104(b) of the Real Property Article, Annotated Code of Maryland provides that, unless otherwise negotiated in the contract or provided by State or local law, the cost of any recordation tax or any State or local Transfer Tax shall be shared equally between the Buyer and Seller.
    **B. FIRST-TIME BUYER.** Under Section 14-104(c) of the Real Property Article, the entire amount of recordation and local transfer tax shall be paid by the Seller of property that is sold to a first-time Maryland homebuyer, unless there is an express agreement that the recordation tax or any state or local transfer tax will not be paid entirely by the Seller.
*RECORDATION AND LOCAL TRANSFER TAX.* If the Buyer is a first-time Maryland homebuyer, Buyer and Seller <u>expressly</u> <u>agree</u>, in accordance with Section 14-104(c) of the Real Property Article, Annotated Code of Maryland, that payment of recordation tax and local transfer tax shall be shared equally between the Buyer and Seller unless a "First-time Maryland Homebuyer Transfer and Recordation Tax Addendum" is attached, which contains a different express agreement.
*STATE TRANSFER TAX:* Under Section 13-203(b) of the Tax-Property Article, Annotated Code of Maryland, the amount of state transfer tax due on the sale of property to a first-time Maryland homebuyer is reduced from 0.50% to 0.25% and shall be paid entirely by the Seller. Buyer is hereby notified that to ensure receipt of the above reduction, Buyer should so indicate on Page 10 of this Contract and complete the required affidavit at settlement indicating that the Buyer is a first-time Maryland homebuyer.

**25. BROKER LIABILITY:** Brokers, their agents, subagents and employees do not assume any responsibility for the condition of the Property or for the performance of this Contract by any or all parties hereto. By signing this Contract, Buyer and Seller acknowledge that they have not relied on any representations made by Brokers, or any agents, subagents or employees of Brokers, except those representations expressly set forth in this Contract.

**26. BROKER'S FEE:** All parties irrevocably instruct the settlement officer to collect the fee or compensation and disburse same according to the terms and conditions provided in the listing agreement and/or agency representation agreement. Settlement shall not be a condition precedent to payment of compensation.

**27. SELLER RESPONSIBILITY:** Seller agrees to keep existing mortgages free of default until settlement. All violation notices or requirements noted or issued by any governmental authority (including without limitation, any permit violation notices), or actions in any court on account thereof, against or affecting the Property at the date of settlement of this Contract, shall be complied with by Seller and the Property conveyed free thereof. The Property is to be held at the risk of Seller until legal title has passed or possession has been given to Buyer. If, prior to the time legal title has passed or possession has been given to Buyer, whichever shall occur first, all or a substantial part of the Property is destroyed or damaged, without fault of Buyer, then this Contract, at the option of Buyer, upon written notice to Seller, shall be null and void and of no further effect, and the deposits shall be disbursed in accordance with the Deposit paragraph of this Contract.

**28. BUYER RESPONSIBILITY:** If Buyer has misrepresented Buyer's financial ability to consummate the purchase of the Property, or if this Contract is contingent upon Buyer securing a written commitment for financing and Buyer fails to apply for such financing within the time period herein specified, or fails to pursue financing diligently and in good faith, or if Buyer makes any misrepresentations in any document relating to financing, or takes (or fails to take) any action which causes Buyer's disqualification for financing, then Buyer shall be in default; and Seller may elect by written notice to Buyer, to terminate this Contract and/or pursue the remedies set forth under the Default paragraph of this Contract.

**29. HOMEOWNER'S ASSOCIATION:** The Property is not part of a development subject to the imposition of mandatory fees as defined by the Maryland Homeowner's Association Act, unless acknowledged by attached addendum.

**30. GROUND RENT:** If the Property is subject to ground rent and the ground rent is not timely paid, the ground lease holder (i.e., the person to whom the ground rent is payable) may bring an action under Section 8-402.3 of the Real Property Article, Annotated Code of Maryland. As a result of this action, a lien may be placed upon the property. If the Property is subject to ground rent, Sections 14-116 and 14-116.1 of the Real Property Article provide the purchaser, upon obtaining ownership of the Property, with certain rights and responsibilities relative to the ground rent. (If the Property is subject to ground rent: See Property Subject to Ground Rent Addendum.)

**31. SALE/SETTLEMENT OR LEASE OF OTHER REAL ESTATE:** Neither this Contract nor the granting of Buyer's loan referred to herein is to be conditioned or contingent in any manner upon the sale, settlement and/or lease of any other real estate unless a contingency for the sale, settlement and/or lease of other real estate is contained in an addendum to this Contract. Unless this Contract is expressly contingent upon the sale, settlement and/or lease of any other real estate, Buyer shall neither apply for nor accept a financing loan commitment which is contingent upon or requires as a pre-condition to funding that any other real estate be sold, settled and/or leased.

**32. LEASES:** Seller may neither negotiate new leases nor renew existing leases for the Property which extend beyond settlement or possession date without Buyer's written consent.

**33. DEFAULT:** Buyer and Seller are required and agree to make full settlement in accordance with the terms of this Contract and acknowledge that failure to do so constitutes a breach hereof. If Buyer fails to make full settlement or is in default due to Buyer's failure to comply with the terms, covenants and conditions of this Contract, the initial Deposit and additional Deposits (the "Deposit") may be retained by Seller as long as a Release of Deposit Agreement is signed and executed by all parties, expressing that said Deposit may be retained by Seller. In the event the parties do not agree to execute a Release of Deposit Agreement, Buyer and Seller shall have all legal and equitable remedies. If Seller fails to make full settlement or is in default due to Seller's failure to comply with the terms, covenants and conditions of this Contract, Buyer shall be entitled to pursue such rights and remedies as may be available, at law or in equity, including, without limitation, an action for specific performance of this Contract and/or monetary damages. In the event of any litigation or dispute between Buyer and Seller concerning the release of the Deposit, Broker's sole responsibility may be met, at Broker's option, by paying the Deposit into the court in which such litigation is pending, or by paying the Deposit into the court of proper jurisdiction by an action of interpleader. Buyer and Seller agree that, upon Broker's payment of the Deposit into the court, neither Buyer nor Seller shall have any further right, claim, demand or action against Broker regarding the release of the Deposit; and Buyer and Seller, jointly and severally, shall indemnify and hold Broker harmless from any and all such rights, claims, demands or actions. In the event of such dispute and election by Broker to file an action of interpleader as herein provided, Buyer and Seller further agree and hereby expressly and irrevocably authorize Broker to deduct from the Deposit all costs incurred by Broker in the filing and maintenance of such action of interpleader including but not limited to filing fees, court costs, service of process fees and attorneys' fees, provided that the amount deducted shall not exceed the lesser of $500 or the amount of the Deposit held by Broker. All such fees and costs authorized herein to be deducted may be deducted by Broker from the Deposit prior to paying the balance of the Deposit to the court. Buyer and Seller further agree and expressly declare that all such fees and costs so deducted shall be the exclusive property of Broker. If the amount deducted by Broker is less than the total of all of the costs incurred by Broker in filing and maintaining the interpleader action, then Buyer and Seller jointly, and severally, agree to reimburse Broker for all such excess costs upon the conclusion of the interpleader action.

**34. MEDIATION OF DISPUTES:** Mediation is a process by which the parties attempt to resolve a dispute or claim with the assistance of a neutral mediator who is authorized to facilitate the resolution of the dispute. The mediator has no authority to make an award, to impose a resolution of the dispute or claim upon the parties or to require the parties to continue mediation if the parties do not desire to do so. Buyer and Seller agree that any dispute or claim arising out of or from this Contract or the transaction which is the subject of this Contract shall be mediated through the Maryland Association of REALTORS®, Inc. or its member local boards/associations in accordance with the established Mediation Rules and Guidelines of the Association or through such other mediator or mediation service as mutually agreed upon by Buyer and Seller, in writing. Unless otherwise agreed in writing by the parties, mediation fees, costs and expenses shall be divided and paid equally by the parties to the mediation. If either party elects to have an attorney present that party shall pay his or her own attorney's fees.

Buyer and Seller further agree that the obligation of Buyer and Seller to mediate as herein provided shall apply to all disputes or claims arising whether prior to, during or within one (1) year following the actual contract settlement date or when settlement should have occurred. Buyer and Seller agree that neither party shall commence any action in any court regarding a dispute or claim arising out of or from this Contract or the transaction which is the subject of this Contract, without first mediating the dispute or claim, unless the right to pursue such action or the ability to protect an interest or pursue a remedy as provided in this Contract, would be precluded by the delay of the mediation. In the event the right to pursue such action, or the ability to protect an interest or pursue a remedy would be precluded by the delay, Buyer or Seller may commence the action only if the initial pleading or document commencing such action is accompanied by a request to stay the proceeding pending the conclusion of the mediation. If a party initiates or commences an action in violation of this provision, the party agrees to pay all costs and expenses, including reasonable attorneys' fees, incurred by the other party to enforce the obligation as provided herein. The provisions of this paragraph shall survive closing and shall not be deemed to have been extinguished by merger with the deed.

**35. ATTORNEY'S FEES:** In any action or proceeding between Buyer and Seller based, in whole or in part, upon the performance or non-performance of the terms and conditions of this Contract, including, but not limited to, breach of contract, negligence, misrepresentation or fraud, the prevailing party in such action or proceeding shall be entitled to receive reasonable attorney's fees from the other party as determined by the court or arbitrator. In any action or proceeding between Buyer and Seller and/or between Buyer and Broker(s) and/or Seller and Broker(s) resulting in Broker(s) being made a party to such action or proceeding, including, but not limited to, any litigation, arbitration, or complaint and claim before the Maryland Real Estate Commission, whether as defendant, cross-defendant, third-party defendant or respondent, Buyer and Seller jointly and severally, agree to indemnify and hold Broker(s) harmless from and against any and all liability, loss, cost, damages or expenses (including filing fees, court costs, service of process fees, transcript fees and attorneys' fees) incurred by Broker(s) in such action or proceeding, providing that such action or proceeding does not result in a judgment against Broker(s).

As used in this Contract, the term "Broker(s)" shall mean: (a) the two (2) Brokers as identified on Page 10 of this Contract; (b) the two (2) named Sales Associates identified on Page 10 of the Contract; and (c) any agent, subagent, salesperson, independent contractor and/or employees of Broker(s). The term "Broker(s)" shall also mean, in the singular, any or either of the named Broker(s) and/or Sales Associate(s) as identified or, in the plural, both of the named Brokers and/or Sales Associates as identified.

This Paragraph shall apply to any and all such action(s) or proceeding(s) against Broker(s) including those action(s) or proceeding(s) based, in whole or in part, upon any alleged act(s) or omission(s) by Broker(s), including, but not limited to, any alleged act of misrepresentation, fraud, non-disclosure, negligence, violation of any statutory or common law duty, or breach of fiduciary duty by Broker(s). The provision of this Paragraph shall survive closing and shall not be deemed to have been extinguished by merger with the deed.

**36. NOTICE OF BUYER'S RIGHT TO SELECT SETTLEMENT SERVICE PROVIDERS:** Buyer has the right to select Buyer's own title insurance company, title lawyer, settlement company, escrow company, mortgage lender or financial institution as defined in the Financial Institutions Article, Annotated Code of Maryland. Buyer acknowledges that Seller may not be prohibited from offering owner financing as a condition of settlement.

**37. PROPERTY OWNER'S TITLE INSURANCE:** Buyer, at Buyer's expense, may purchase owner's title insurance at either "standard" or "enhanced" coverage and rates. The coverage afforded by such title insurance would be governed by the terms and conditions thereof, and the premium for obtaining such title insurance coverage would be determined by the extent of its coverage. For purposes of owner's title insurance policy premium rate disclosures by Buyer's lender, Buyer and Seller agree that enhanced rates (if available) shall be quoted by Buyer's lender. Buyer understands that nothing herein obligates Buyer to obtain any owner's title insurance coverage at any time, including at settlement, and that the availability of owner's title insurance coverage is subject to the underwriting criteria of the title insurer.

**38. LIMITED WARRANTY:** NOTICE TO BUYER: IF A WARRANTY PLAN IS BEING OFFERED WITH THE PURCHASE OF THE PROPERTY, IT MAY BE A LIMITED WARRANTY. SINCE SUCH WARRANTY PLANS DO NOT COVER STRUCTURAL DEFECTS AND MAY NOT COVER PRE-EXISTING DEFECTS, BUYER SHOULD REQUEST THE REAL ESTATE AGENT TO PROVIDE BUYER WITH ANY BROCHURE WHICH DESCRIBES THE PLAN IN ORDER TO DETERMINE THE EXTENT OF COVERAGE PROVIDED BY THE WARRANTY.

**39. PROPERTY INSURANCE BROCHURE:** An informational brochure published by the Maryland Association of REALTORS®, Inc. titled "The New Reality of Property Insurance – What You Should Know" is available to explain current issues relative to obtaining insurance coverage for the Property to be purchased.

**40. FLOOD DISCLOSURE NOTICE:**
**A. FLOOD INSURANCE PREMIUMS:** The Property or part of the Property may be located in an area established by the government as a "flood plain" or otherwise in an area where flood insurance could be required by Buyer's mortgage lender as a condition of granting a mortgage. In addition, construction on the Property could be prohibited or restricted.

The National Flood Insurance Program ("NFIP") provides for the availability of flood insurance but also establishes flood insurance policy premiums based on the risk of flooding in the area where properties are located. Due to amendments to federal law governing the NFIP those premiums are increasing, and in some cases will rise by a substantial amount over the premiums previously charged for flood insurance. As a result, Buyer should not rely on the premiums paid for flood insurance on the Property as an indication of the premiums that will apply after Buyer completes the purchase. In considering the purchase of this Property, Buyer should consult with one or more carriers of flood insurance for better understanding of flood insurance coverage, the premiums that are likely to be required to purchase such insurance and any available information about how those premiums may increase in the future. Detailed information regarding flood insurance coverage may be obtained at: http://www.fema.gov/flood-insurance-reform-act-2012.

**B. FLOOD INSURANCE RATE MAPS:** The State of Maryland in conjunction with the Federal Emergency Management Agency has been systematically updating flood insurance rate maps. The Property may be affected. Buyer is advised to contact the Maryland Department of the Environment and consult a flood insurance carrier to inquire about the status of the Property. Detailed information regarding updated maps may be obtained at: http://www.mdfloodmaps.net/home.html.

**41. GUARANTY FUND:** NOTICE TO BUYER: BUYER IS PROTECTED BY THE REAL ESTATE GUARANTY FUND OF THE MARYLAND REAL ESTATE COMMISSION, UNDER SECTION 17-404 OF THE BUSINESS OCCUPATIONS AND PROFESSIONS ARTICLE OF THE ANNOTATED CODE OF MARYLAND, FOR LOSSES IN AN AMOUNT NOT EXCEEDING $50,000 FOR ANY CLAIM.

**42. SINGLE FAMILY RESIDENTIAL REAL PROPERTY DISCLOSURE NOTICE:** Buyer is advised of the right to receive a "Disclosure and Disclaimer Statement" from Seller (Section 10-702 Real Property Article, Annotated Code of Maryland).

**43. MARYLAND NON-RESIDENT SELLER:** If the Property is not the Seller's principal residence and the Seller is a non-resident individual of the State of Maryland or is a non-resident entity which is not formed under the laws of the State of Maryland or qualified to do business in the State of Maryland, a withholding tax from the proceeds of sale may be withheld at the time of settlement except as otherwise provided by Maryland law. (See Maryland Non-Resident Seller Transfer Withholding Tax Addendum.)

**44. INTERNAL REVENUE SERVICE FILING:** Buyer and Seller each agree to cooperate with the settlement officer by providing all necessary information so that a report can be filed with the Internal Revenue Service, as required by Section 6045 of the IRS Code. To the extent permitted by law, any fees incurred as a result of such filing will be paid by the Seller.

**45. NOTICE TO BUYER CONCERNING THE CHESAPEAKE AND ATLANTIC COASTAL BAYS CRITICAL AREA:** Buyer is advised that all or a portion of the property may be located in the "Critical Area" of the Chesapeake and Atlantic Coastal Bays, and that additional zoning, land use, and resource protection regulations apply in this area. The "Critical Area" generally consists of all land and water areas within 1,000 feet beyond the landward boundaries of state or private wetlands, the Chesapeake Bay, the Atlantic Coastal Bays, and all of their tidal tributaries. The "Critical Area" also includes the waters of and lands under the Chesapeake Bay, the Atlantic Coastal Bays and all of their tidal tributaries to the head of tide. For information as to whether the property is located within the Critical Area, Buyer may contact the local Department of Planning and Zoning, which maintains maps showing the extent of the Critical Area in the jurisdiction. Allegany, Carroll, Frederick, Garrett, Howard, Montgomery and Washington Counties do not include land located in the Critical Area.

**46. WETLANDS NOTICE:** Buyer is advised that if the Property being purchased contains waters of the United States, or if the Property contains land and/or waters regulated by the State, including, but not limited to, wetlands, approval from the U.S. Army Corps of Engineers (Corps) and/or the Maryland Department of the Environment (MDE) will be necessary before starting any work, including construction, if the work includes the discharge of dredged or fill material into a regulated area, or certain other activities conducted in a regulated area. The Corps has adopted a broad definition of waters of the United States, which occur throughout the Chesapeake Bay Region, as well as other portions of the State. The land and waters regulated by the State include tidal wetlands, nontidal wetlands and their buffers, and streams and their 100-year nontidal floodplain. For information as to whether the Property includes waters of the United States or land and/or waters regulated by the State, Buyer may contact the Baltimore District of the Corps and/or MDE. Buyer may also elect, at Buyer's expense, to engage the services of a qualified specialist to inspect the Property for the presence of Corps- or MDE-regulated areas, including wetlands, prior to submitting a written offer to purchase the Property; or Buyer may include in Buyer's written offer a clause making Buyer's purchase of the Property contingent upon a satisfactory wetlands inspection.

**47. FOREST CONSERVATION ACT NOTICE:** If the Property is a tract of land 40,000 square feet or more in size, Buyer is notified that, unless exempted by applicable law, as a prerequisite to any subdivision plan or grading or sediment control permit for the Property, Buyer will be required to comply with the provisions of the Maryland Forest Conservation Act imposed by Section 5-1601, et seq. of the Natural Resources Article, Annotated Code of Maryland, including, among other things, the submission and acceptance of a Forest Stand Delineation and a Forest Conservation Plan for the Property in accordance with applicable laws and regulations. Unless otherwise expressly set forth in an addendum to this Contract, Seller represents and warrants that the Property is not currently subject to a Forest Conservation Plan, Management Agreement or any other pending obligation binding the owner of the Property under said Act; further, Seller represents and warrants that no activities have been undertaken on the Property by Seller in violation of the Forest Conservation Act.

**48. NOTICE CONCERNING CONSERVATION EASEMENTS:** If the Property is encumbered by a Conservation Easement as defined in Section 10-705 of the Real Property Article, Annotated Code of Maryland, the contract must contain a notice concerning the easement, which is contained in an attached addendum. This Paragraph does not apply to the sale of property in an action to foreclose a mortgage or deed of trust. (If the Property is encumbered by a Conservation Easement: See Conservation Easement Addendum.)

**49. FOREIGN INVESTMENT TAXES-FIRPTA:** Section 1445 of the United States Internal Revenue Code of 1986 provides that a Buyer of residential real property located in the United States must withhold federal income taxes from the payment of the purchase price if (a) the purchase price exceeds Three Hundred Thousand Dollars ($300,000.00) and (b) the seller is a foreign person. Unless otherwise stated in an addendum attached hereto, if the purchase price is in excess of Three Hundred Thousand Dollars ($300,000.00), Seller represents that Seller is not a non-resident alien, foreign corporation, foreign partnership, foreign trust or foreign estate (as those terms are defined by the Internal Revenue Code and applicable regulations) and agrees to execute an affidavit to this effect at the time of settlement.

**50. CRIMINAL ACTIVITY AND SEXUAL OFFENDERS:** Buyer may contact the state, county or municipal police departments in which the Property is located or check the "Sex Offender Registry" at the Maryland Department of Public Safety and Correctional Services website in order to ascertain criminal activity in the vicinity of the Property or the presence of registered sexual offenders who live or work within the vicinity of the Property. Buyer acknowledges that Buyer is solely responsible to inquire of such matters before signing this Contract. Buyer shall have no right to cancel this Contract based upon criminal activity or the presence of registered sexual offenders in the vicinity of the Property. Buyer further acknowledges that no real estate licensee involved in the sale or purchase of the Property, whether acting as the agent for Seller or Buyer, has any duty nor assumes any duty or responsibility to ascertain criminal activity or the presence of registered sexual offenders in the vicinity of the Property.

**51. MILITARY INSTALLATIONS:** This Section does not apply in Allegany, Carroll, Frederick, Garrett, Howard, Montgomery, and Washington Counties. Buyer is advised that the Property may be located near a military installation that conducts flight operations, munitions testing, or military operations that may result in high noise levels.

**52. NOTICE TO THE PARTIES:**
　　(A) NO REPRESENTATIONS: Brokers, their agents, subagents and employees, make no representations with respect to:
　　　　(1) Water quantity, quality, color, or taste or operating conditions of public and/or private water systems;
　　　　(2) Location, size or operating condition of on-site sewage disposal systems;
　　　　(3) The extensions of public utilities by local municipal authorities, existence or availability of public utilities, and any assessments, fees or costs for public utilities which might be imposed by local municipal authorities or private entities, should public utilities be extended or available to the subject Property. (Buyer should consult the Department of Public Works to determine the availability of proposed future extensions of utilities.);
　　　　(4) Lot size and exact location. If the subject Property is part of a recorded subdivision, Buyer can review the plat upon request at the Record Office. If the subject Property is not part of a recorded subdivision, Buyer may verify exact size and location through a survey by a licensed engineer or land surveyor, at Buyer's expense;
　　　　(5) Existing zoning or permitted uses of the Property, including, without limitation, whether any improvements to the Property required permit(s) and, if so, whether such improvements, were completed pursuant to permit(s) issued and/or whether any permit(s) issued were complied with. Buyer should contact the appropriate local government agency and/or a licensed engineer to verify zoning, permit issuance/status, and permitted uses; or
　　　　(6) Whether properly licensed contractors have been used to make repairs, renovations and improvements to the Property.
　　(B) NO ADVISING: Brokers/agents are not advising the parties as to certain other issues, including without limitation: soil conditions; flood hazard areas; possible restrictions of the use of property due to restrictive covenants, subdivision, environmental laws, easements or other documents; airport or aircraft noise; planned land use, roads or highways; and construction materials and/or hazardous materials, including without limitation flame retardant treated plywood (FRT), radon, radium, mold spores, urea formaldehyde foam insulation (UFFI), synthetic stucco (EIFS), asbestos, polybutylene piping and lead-based paint. Information relating to these issues may be available from appropriate governmental authorities. This disclosure is not intended to provide an inspection contingency.
　　(C) COMPENSATION OF VENDORS: Buyer and Seller each assume full responsibility for selecting and compensating their respective vendors.
　　(D) PROTECTION OF HOMEOWNERS IN FORECLOSURE ACT NOTICE: BUYER AND SELLER ACKNOWLEDGE THAT, UNDER SECTION 7-310 OF THE REAL PROPERTY ARTICLE OF THE ANNOTATED CODE OF MARYLAND, IF THE MORTGAGE ON THE PROPERTY IS AT LEAST 60 DAYS IN DEFAULT ON THE DATE OF CONTRACT ACCEPTANCE, SELLER HAS THE RIGHT TO RESCIND THE CONTRACT WITHIN 5 DAYS AFTER THE DATE OF CONTRACT ACCEPTANCE. ANY PROVISION IN THIS CONTRACT OR OTHER AGREEMENT THAT ATTEMPTS OR PURPORTS TO WAIVE ANY OF THE SELLER'S RIGHTS UNDER SECTION 7-310 IS VOID.

**53. PROPERTY TAX NOTICE - 60 DAY APPEAL:** If any real property is transferred after January 1 and before the beginning of the next taxable year to a new owner, the new owner may submit a written appeal as to a value or classification on or before 60 days after the date of the transfer.

**54. NON-ASSIGNABILITY:** This Contract may not be assigned without the written consent of Buyer and Seller. If Buyer and Seller agree in writing to an assignment of this Contract, the original parties to this Contract remain obligated hereunder until settlement.

**55. PARAGRAPH HEADINGS:** The Paragraph headings of this Contract are for convenience and reference only, and in no way define or limit the intent, rights or obligations of the parties.

**56. COMPUTATION OF DAYS:** As used in this Contract, and in any addendum or addenda to this Contract, the term "days" shall mean consecutive calendar days, including Saturdays, Sundays, and holidays, whether federal, state, local or religious. A day shall be measured from 12:00:01 a.m. to and including 11:59:59 p.m. E.S.T. For the purposes of calculating days, the count of "days" shall begin on the day following the day upon which any act or notice as provided in this Contract, or any addendum or addenda to this Contract, was required to be performed or made.

**57. ENTIRE AGREEMENT:** This Contract and any addenda thereto contain the final and entire agreement between the parties, and neither they nor their agents shall be bound by any terms, conditions, statements, warranties or representations, oral or written, not herein contained. The parties to this Contract mutually agree that it is binding upon them, their heirs, executors, administrators, personal representatives, successors and, if permitted as herein provided, assigns. Once signed, the terms of this Contract can only be changed by a document executed by all parties. This Contract shall be interpreted and construed in accordance with the laws of the State of Maryland. It is further agreed that this Contract may be executed in counterparts, each of which when considered together shall constitute the original Contract.

Buyer _____ / _____　　　　　　　　Page 9 of 10　10/15　　　　　　　　Seller _____ / _____

MARYLAND RESIDENTIAL PROPERTY DISCLOSURE AND DISCLAIMER STATEMENT

Property Address: _____

Legal Description: _____

### NOTICE TO SELLER AND PURCHASER

Section 10-702 of the Real Property Article, *Annotated Code of Maryland*, requires the owner of certain residential real property to furnish to the purchaser either (a) a RESIDENTIAL PROPERTY DISCLAIMER STATEMENT stating that the owner is selling the property "as is" and makes no representations or warranties as to the condition of the property or any improvements on the real property, except as otherwise provided in the contract of sale, or in a listing of latent defects; or (b) a RESIDENTIAL PROPERTY DISCLOSURE STATEMENT disclosing defects or other information about the condition of the real property actually known by the owner. Certain transfers of residential property are excluded from this requirement (see the exemptions listed below).

10-702. EXEMPTIONS. The following are specifically excluded from the provisions of §10-702:

1. The initial sale of single family residential real property:
   A. that has never been occupied; or
   B. for which a certificate of occupancy has been issued within 1 year before the seller and buyer enter into a contract of sale;
2. A transfer that is exempt from the transfer tax under §13-207 of the Tax-Property Article, except land installment contracts of sales under §13-207(a)(11) of the Tax-Property Article and options to purchase real property under §13-207(a)(12) of the Tax-Property Article;
3. A sale by a lender or an affiliate or subsidiary of a lender that acquired the real property by foreclosure or deed in lieu of foreclosure;
4. A sheriff's sale, tax sale, or sale by foreclosure, partition, or by court appointed trustee;
5. A transfer by a fiduciary in the course of the administration of a decedent's estate, guardianship, conservatorship, or trust;
6. A transfer of single family residential real property to be converted by the buyer into use other than residential use or to be demolished; or
7. A sale of unimproved real property.

Section 10-702 also requires the owner to disclose information about latent defects in the property that the owner has actual knowledge of. The owner must provide this information even if selling the property "as is." "Latent defects" are defined as: Material defects in real property or an improvement to real property that:

(1) A purchaser would not reasonably be expected to ascertain or observe by a careful visual inspection of the real property; and
(2) Would pose a direct threat to the health or safety of:
   (i) the purchaser; or
   (ii) an occupant of the real property, including a tenant or invitee of the purchaser.

### MARYLAND RESIDENTIAL PROPERTY DISCLOSURE STATEMENT

NOTICE TO OWNERS: Complete and sign this statement only if you elect to disclose defects, including latent defects, or other information about the condition of the property actually known by you; otherwise, sign the Residential Property Disclaimer Statement. You may wish to obtain professional advice or inspections of the property; however, you are not required to undertake or provide any independent investigation or inspection of the property in order to make the disclosure set forth below. The disclosure is based on your personal knowledge of the condition of the property at the time of the signing of this statement.

NOTICE TO PURCHASERS: The information provided is the representation of the Owners and is based upon the actual knowledge of Owners as of the date noted. Disclosure by the Owners is not a substitute for an inspection by an independent home inspection company, and you may wish to obtain such an inspection. The information contained in this statement is not a warranty by the Owners as to the condition of the property of which the Owners have no knowledge or other conditions of which the Owners have no actual knowledge.

How long have you owned the property?_____

**Property System: Water, Sewage, Heating & Air Conditioning (Answer all that apply)**

| | | | | | |
|---|---|---|---|---|---|
| Water Supply | ❏ Public | ❏ Well | ❏ Other _____ | | |
| Sewage Disposal | ❏ Public | | ❏ Septic System approved for _____ (# bedrooms) **Other Type** _____ | | |
| Garbage Disposal | ❏ Yes | ❏ No | | | |
| Dishwasher | ❏ Yes | ❏ No | | | |
| Heating | ❏ Oil | ❏ Natural Gas | ❏ Electric | ❏ Heat Pump Age _____ | ❏ Other _____ |
| Air Conditioning | ❏ Oil | ❏ Natural Gas | ❏ Electric | ❏ Heat Pump Age _____ | ❏ Other _____ |
| Hot Water | ❏ Oil | ❏ Natural Gas | ❏ Electric Capacity _____ Age _____ | | ❏ Other _____ |

**Please indicate your actual knowledge with respect to the following:**

1. Foundation: Any settlement or other problems? ❑ Yes ❑ No ❑ Unknown
Comments: _____

2. Basement: Any leaks or evidence of moisture? ❑ Yes ❑ No ❑ Unknown ❑ Does Not Apply
Comments: _____

3. Roof: Any leaks or evidence of moisture? ❑ Yes ❑ No ❑ Unknown
   Type of Roof: _____ Age _____
Comments: _____
   Is there any existing fire retardant treated plywood? ❑ Yes ❑ No ❑ Unknown
Comments: _____

4. Other Structural Systems, including exterior walls and floors:
Comments: _____
   Any defects (structural or otherwise)? ❑ Yes ❑ No ❑ Unknown
Comments: _____

5. Plumbing System: Is the system in operating condition? ❑ Yes ❑ No ❑ Unknown
Comments: _____

6. Heating Systems: Is heat supplied to all finished rooms? ❑ Yes ❑ No ❑ Unknown
Comments: _____
   Is the system in operating condition? ❑ Yes ❑ No ❑ Unknown
Comments: _____

7. Air Conditioning System: Is cooling supplied to all finished rooms? ❑ Yes ❑ No ❑ Unknown ❑ Does Not Apply
Comments: _____
   Is the system in operating condition? ❑ Yes ❑ No ❑ Unknown ❑ Does Not Apply
Comments: _____

8. Electric Systems: Are there any problems with electrical fuses, circuit breakers, outlets or wiring?
   ❑ Yes ❑ No ❑ Unknown
Comments: _____

**8A. Will the smoke alarms provide an alarm in the event of a power outage?** ❑ Yes ❑ No
**Are the smoke alarms over 10 years old?** ❑ Yes ❑ No
**If the smoke alarms are battery operated, are they sealed, tamper resistant units incorporating a silence/hush button, which use long-life batteries as required in all Maryland Homes by 2018?** ❑ Yes ❑ No
**Comments:** _____

9. Septic Systems: Is the septic system functioning properly? ❑ Yes ❑ No ❑ Unknown ❑ Does Not Apply
   When was the system last pumped? Date _____ ❑ Unknown
Comments: _____

10. Water Supply: Any problem with water supply? ❑ Yes ❑ No ❑ Unknown
Comments: _____
   Home water treatment system: ❑ Yes ❑ No ❑ Unknown
Comments: _____
   Fire sprinkler system: ❑ Yes ❑ No ❑ Unknown ❑ Does Not Apply
Comments: _____
   Are the systems in operating condition? ❑ Yes ❑ No ❑ Unknown
Comments: _____

11. Insulation:
   In exterior walls? ❑ Yes ❑ No ❑ Unknown
   In ceiling/attic? ❑ Yes ❑ No ❑ Unknown
   In any other areas? ❑ Yes ❑ No Where?_____
Comments: _____

12. Exterior Drainage: Does water stand on the property for more than 24 hours after a heavy rain?
   ❑ Yes ❑ No ❑ Unknown
Comments: _____
   Are gutters and downspouts in good repair? ❑ Yes ❑ No ❑ Unknown
Comments: _____

13. Wood-destroying insects: Any infestation and/or prior damage? ❏ Yes ❏ No ❏ Unknown
Comments: _____

| | | | | |
|---|---|---|---|---|
| Any treatments or repairs? | ❏ Yes | ❏ No | ❏ Unknown | |
| Any warranties? | ❏ Yes | ❏ No | ❏ Unknown | |

Comments: _____

14. Are there any hazardous or regulated materials (including, but not limited to, licensed landfills, asbestos, radon gas, lead-based paint, underground storage tanks, or other contamination) on the property? ❏ Yes ❏ No ❏ Unknown
If yes, specify below
Comments: _____

15. If the property relies on the combustion of a fossil fuel for heat, ventilation, hot water, or clothes dryer operation, is a carbon monoxide alarm installed in the property?
❏ Yes ❏ No ❏ Unknown
Comments: _____

16. Are there any zoning violations, nonconforming uses, violation of building restrictions or setback requirements or any recorded or unrecorded easement, except for utilities, on or affecting the property? ❏ Yes ❏ No ❏ Unknown
If yes, specify below
Comments: _____

**16A. If you or a contractor have made improvements to the property, were the required permits pulled from the county or local permitting office?** ❏ Yes ❏ No ❏ Does Not Apply ❏ Unknown
**Comments:** _____

17. Is the property located in a flood zone, conservation area, wetland area, Chesapeake Bay critical area or Designated Historic District? ❏ Yes ❏ No ❏ Unknown If yes, specify below
Comments: _____

18. Is the property subject to any restriction imposed by a Home Owners Association or any other type of community association?
❏ Yes ❏ No ❏ Unknown If yes, specify below
Comments: _____

19. Are there any other material defects, including latent defects, affecting the physical condition of the property?
❏ Yes ❏ No ❏ Unknown
Comments: _____

NOTE: Owner(s) may wish to disclose the condition of other buildings on the property on a separate RESIDENTIAL PROPERTY DISCLOSURE STATEMENT.

The owner(s) acknowledge having carefully examined this statement, including any comments, and verify that it is complete and accurate as of the date signed. The owner(s) further acknowledge that they have been informed of their rights and obligations under §10-702 of the Maryland Real Property Article.

Owner _____ Date _____

Owner _____ Date _____

The purchaser(s) acknowledge receipt of a copy of this disclosure statement and further acknowledge that they have been informed of their rights and obligations under §10-702 of the Maryland Real Property Article.

Purchaser _____ Date _____

Purchaser _____ Date _____

### MARYLAND RESIDENTIAL PROPERTY DISCLAIMER STATEMENT

NOTICE TO OWNER(S): Sign this statement only if you elect to sell the property without representations and warranties as to its condition, except as otherwise provided in the contract of sale and in the listing of latent defects set forth below; otherwise, complete and sign the RESIDENTIAL PROPERTY DISCLOSURE STATEMENT.

Except for the latent defects listed below, the undersigned owner(s) of the real property make no representations or warranties as to the condition of the real property or any improvements thereon, and the purchaser will be receiving the real property "as is" with all defects, including latent defects, which may exist, except as otherwise provided in the real estate contract of sale. The owner(s) acknowledge having carefully examined this statement and further acknowledge that they have been informed of their rights and obligations under §10-702 of the Maryland Real Property Article.

The owner(s) has actual knowledge of the following latent defects: _____

_____

_____

Owner _____ Date _____

Owner _____ Date _____

The purchaser(s) acknowledge receipt of a copy of this disclaimer statement and further acknowledge that they have been informed of their rights and obligations under §10-702 of the Maryland Real Property Article.

Purchaser _____ Date _____

Purchaser _____ Date _____

FORM: MREC/DLLR: Rev 8/30/2013

**DISCLOSURE OF INFORMATION ON LEAD-BASED PAINT AND/OR LEAD-BASED PAINT HAZARDS**

MARYLAND
ASSOCIATION OF
REALTORS®

**Property Address:** _____

SELLER REPRESENTS AND WARRANTS, INTENDING THAT SUCH BE RELIED UPON REGARDING THE ABOVE PROPERTY, THAT
(**SELLER TO INITIAL APPLICABLE LINE**): _____ / _____ housing was constructed prior to 1978 **OR** _____ / _____
date of construction is uncertain.

**FEDERAL LEAD WARNING STATEMENT**: A buyer/tenant of any interest in residential real property on which a residential dwelling was built prior to 1978 is notified that such property may contain lead-based paint and that exposure to lead from lead-based paint, paint chips or lead paint dust may place young children at risk of developing lead poisoning if not managed properly. Lead poisoning in young children may produce permanent neurological damage, including learning disabilities, reduced intelligence quotient, behavioral problems, and impaired memory. Lead poisoning also poses a particular risk to pregnant women. The seller/landlord of any interest in residential real property is required to disclose to the buyer/tenant the presence of known lead-based paint hazards and to provide the buyer/tenant with any information on lead-based paint hazards from risk assessments or inspections in the seller's/landlord's possession. A **tenant** must receive a federally approved pamphlet on lead poisoning prevention. It is recommended that a **buyer** conduct a risk assessment or inspection for possible lead-based paint hazards prior to purchase.

**Seller's/Landlord's Disclosure**

(a) Presence of lead-based paint and/or lead-based paint hazards (initial (i) or (ii) below):
    (i) _____ / _____ Known lead-based paint and/or lead-based paint hazards are present in the housing (explain).
    _____
    _____

    (ii) _____ / _____ Seller/Landlord has no knowledge of lead-based paint and/or lead-based paint hazards in the housing.
(b) Records and reports available to the seller (initial (i) or (ii) below):

    (i) _____ / _____ Seller/Landlord has provided the purchaser/tenant with all available records and reports pertaining to lead-based paint and/or lead-based paint hazards in the housing (list documents below).
    _____
    _____

    (ii) _____ / _____ Seller/Landlord has no reports or records pertaining to lead-based paint and/or lead-based paint hazards in the housing.

**Buyer's/Tenant's Acknowledgment** (initial)

(c) _____ / _____ Buyer/Tenant has received copies of all information listed in section (b)(i) above, if any.

(d) _____ / _____ Buyer/Tenant has received the pamphlet Protect Your Family from Lead In Your Home.

**(e) Buyer** has (initial (i) or (ii) below):

    (i) _____ / _____ received a 10-day opportunity (or mutually agreed upon period) to conduct a risk assessment or inspection for the presence of lead-based paint and/or lead-based paint hazards; or

    (ii) _____ / _____ waived the opportunity to conduct a risk assessment or inspection for the presence of lead-based paint and/or lead-based paint hazards.

**Agent's Acknowledgment** (initial)

(f) _____ Agent has informed the Seller/Landlord of the Seller's/Landlord's obligations under 42 U.S.C. 4852(d) and is aware of his/her responsibility to ensure compliance.

**Certification of Accuracy**

The following parties have reviewed the information above and certify, to the best of their knowledge, that the information they have provided is true and accurate.

_____    _____
Seller/Landlord             Date      Buyer/Tenant             Date

_____    _____
Seller/Landlord             Date      Buyer/Tenant             Date

_____    _____
Seller's/Landlord's Agent       Date      Buyer's/Tenant's Agent       Date

10/10

# List of MAR forms

o   AS IS Addendum - 10/15

o   Cash Appraisal Contingency Addendum (MAR) - 10/14

o   Condo Resale Receipt of Documents (MAR) - 10/15

o   Condo. Resale Discl. and Transmittal of Docs. from Seller as Unit Owner (MAR) - 10/13

o   Condo. Resale Discl. Cert. from Council of Unit Owners (7+ units) (MAR) - 10/09

o   Condominium Resale Notice (MAR) - 10/13

o   Consent for Dual Agency - 1/11

o   Conservation Easement Addendum (MAR) - 10/13

o   Conventional Financing Addendum - 10/15

o   Cover Sheet

o   Disclosure of Information on Lead-Based Paint and/or Lead-Based Paint Hazards - 10/10

o   Disclosure of Licensee Status Addendum (MAR) - 10/13

o   FHA Financing Addendum (MAR) - 10/14

o   First-Time MD Home Buyer Transfer and Recordation Tax Add. - (MAR) - 10/13 o     Gift of Funds Addendum (MAR) - 10/13

o     HAFA Addendum to Residential Contract of Sale - 10/13

o     HOA Discl. To Buyer 12 lots Res. (MAR) - 10/13

o     HOA Discl. To Buyer 12 Or Fewer Lots Res. (MAR) - 10/13

o     HOA Initial Sale Discl. and Transmittal of Docs, Non-Res (MAR) - 10/13

o     HOA Initial Sale Notice, more than 12 lots, Res (MAR) - 10/14

o     HOA Initial Sale Notice, Non-Residential (MAR) - 10/13

o     HOA Resale Notice (and Initial Sale, 12 or fewer lots, Res) (MAR) - 10/14

o     HOA Substantial and Material Amndmts - Notice and Discl. (MAR) - 10/13

o     Kickout Addendum (MAR) - 10/13

o     Lease Option Agreement (Option to Purchase) - 10/11

o     Maryland Lead Poisoning Prevention Program Disclosure - 1/15

o     MD Non-Resident Seller Transfer Withholding Tax Addm (MAR) - 10/13 o MD Res Prop Disclosure and Disclaimer Statement - 8/13

o Mutual Release of Obligation Under Contract of Sale - 10/13

o Notice to Buyer and Seller of Buyer's Rights and Sellers Obligations - 10/14

o Notice to Consumer Regarding Service Providers and Contractors - 1/15

o Notification of Dual Agency within a Team

o On-Site Sewage Disp. Sys (OSDS) Insp. and Test Add (MAR) - 10/13

o Property Inspections Addendum (MAR) - 1/15

o Property Inspections Notice - 10/15

o Property Insurance Brochure

o Property Subject to Ground Rent Addendum (MAR) - 10/13

o Protect Your Family From Lead in Your Home Pamphlet - 9/13

o Purchase Price Escalation Add (MAR) - 10/13

o Residential Contract of Sale (MAR) - 10/15

o Sale, Financing, Settlement or Lease of Other R.E. Add (MAR) - 10/13 o    Seller Contribution Addendum - 10/14

o    Short Sale Addendum - 10/13

o    Statement About Tenancy (MAR) - 10/13

o    Third Party Approval Addendum (MAR) - 10/13

o    Understanding Whom Real Estate Agents Represent #1- 1/11

o    Understanding Whom Real Estate Agents Represent #2- 1/11

o    Understanding Whom Real Estate Agents Represent #3- 1/11

o    Understanding Whom Real Estate Agents Represent #4- 1/11

o    Understanding Whom Real Estate Agents Represent #5- 1/11

o    Unilateral Notice of Termination Under Contract of Sale - 10/13

o    *Unimproved Land Cont Add (MAR) - 10/13*
o    *Unimproved Land Contr of Sale (MAR) - 10/15*
o    *USDA Financing Addendum - 10/15*
o    *VA Financing Addendum (MAR) - 10/14*
o    *Water Quality Addendum (MAR) - 10/13*